Truth is not what you want
it to be; it is what it is,
and you must bend to
its power or live a lie.
Miyamoto Musashi
theWisdomWarrior.com

# The Little Book of Inequalities
*Is it Really Better to Live a Lie?*



Cover design by the author.

DISCLAIMER:
The author has no intention to slight, defame, or offend any person living or dead and apologizes for any factual errors that may unwittingly be presented in these pages.

# The Little Book of In≠qualities
## CONTENTS

# INTRODUCTION

In the late 1980s, one of my martial arts students introduced me to the educational audiotape albums produced by Nightingale-Conant. He let me borrow a few of his albums until I realized that I wanted to own titles he did not have. Besides, I didn't like borrowing books or audio programs since I often dwelt on them and would want to refer to them more frequently than a polite borrowing duration would allow. The first album I purchased was Tony Robbins's 1986 offering *Unlimited Power*, which was his exposition and extension of Bandler and Grinder's Neuro-linguistic Programming.

The revelation that one could reprogram one's own mind via self-talk and other techniques was, in my opinion, an enormous contribution to psychology and especially to the burgeoning field of self-development. But, the idea itself was not new. The Roman emperor and Stoic philosopher Marcus Aurelius (emperor from

161-180 AD) was especially adept at succinctly explaining Bandler and Grinder's point of view, 1800 years before they actually had it.

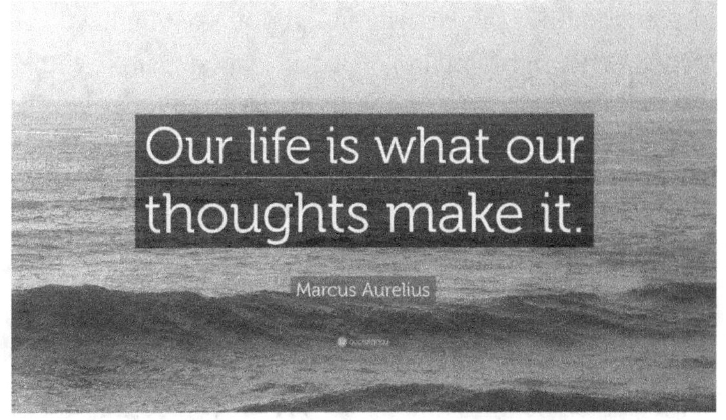


Before Marcus Aurelius, the Greek Stoic philosopher Epectitus (50 – 135 AD) said:

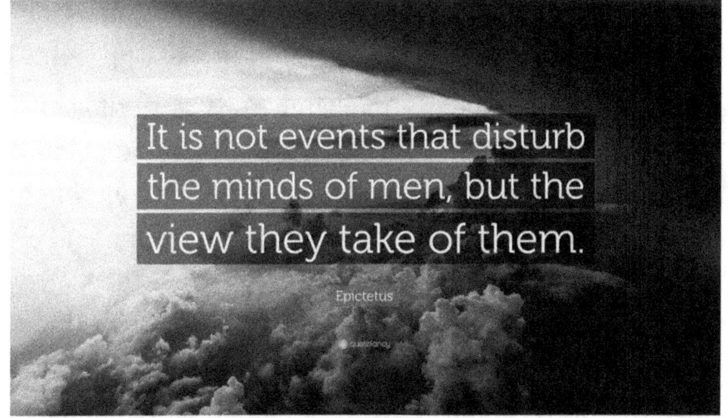


Or, in Tony Robbins's phrasing, "The quality of your life equals the quality of your (self-)communication."

Word-choice tends to affect thinking. Your saying, "I have to take care of the grandkids this afternoon," is a more negative version of "I get to take care of the grandkids this afternoon." If you say you have a "really challenging malady", it feels worse than if you say that you have an "annoying illness". And that is still more dire-sounding than saying that you have a "temporary cold". Thus, the self-improvement coach advocates that people control their own self-talk.

This rather simple concept can help people make large strides in the areas of self-respect, self-control, self-development, and personal responsibility. Self-talk is the person helping him/herself. However, decades before Bandler and Grinder, French Postmodernist philosophers were similarly concerned with language, but not in order for the individual to control his own mind, but to change the way in which we see the world.

Postmodernism is the name for the offerings of several philosophers (Derrida, Foucault, Lyotard, et al.), who worked along similar philosophical lines, although each has his own specific contribution. They contend that since every concept has myriad meanings depending on several factors, one "meaning" is as good as another. Since your description of a meaning depends upon the words you use, words are important in delivering that meaning. All language is generated from cultural roots, they aver, but because language is rendered via such a personal process, he/she who generates it may know its intended meaning, but others do not, and perhaps cannot. Both logic and evidence are as cultural-specific and as subjective as language. Therefore, nothing can be actually proven decisively or objectively. Personal feelings are not verbal and thus are "deeper" than logic. Because they are deeper, they are surer than either logic or evidence. Thus Postmodernism, although preceding Neuro-linguistic Programming, uses similar ideas albeit not for personal development. Rather, the exponents of Postmodernism attempt to foist their preferred words, their preferred thoughts, on everyone else, claiming that their personal feelings (a superior method of understanding) cannot be logical refuted.

The ancestors of Postmodernism, in my opinion, were two philosophers and a scientist.

Jean-Jacques Rousseau (1712-1778) felt that humankind's original sin was its unique ability to reason. Because of reason, we no longer lived in harmony with nature as did other animals. Rousseau continued his theme by suggesting that rationality led humankind to develop excess wealth, which in turn led to property rights, which in turn lead to jealousy and contention. He claimed that humans were fundamentally passionate rather than rational.

He alleged that his "felt" position—that God's existence was the root of all explanations—could not be reasoned away from him. By extension, religion was important to a culture; thus, although the state could not compel anyone to believe, it could banish citizens for "antisocial" behavior—behavior such as refusing to sacrifice as a social duty, as one might in a religion.

Immanuel Kant (1724-1804), contrarily, seemed to support objective reason.

Kant...argued that the supreme principle of morality is a principle of practical rationality that he dubbed the "Categorical Imperative" (CI) ["Act such that you may wish your actions to be a standard that all others follow"]. Kant characterized the CI as an objective, rationally necessary and unconditional principle that we must follow despite any natural desires we may have to the contrary. All specific moral requirements, according to Kant, are justified by this principle, which means that all immoral actions are irrational because they violate the CI. Other philosophers, such as Hobbes, Locke and Aquinas, had also argued that moral requirements are based on standards of rationality. However, these standards were either instrumental principles of rationality for satisfying one's desires, as in Hobbes, or external rational principles that are discoverable by reason, as in Locke and Aquinas. Kant agreed with many of his predecessors that an analysis of practical reason reveals the requirement that rational agents must conform to instrumental principles. Yet he also argued that conformity to the CI (a non-instrumental principle), and hence to moral requirements themselves, can nevertheless be shown to be essential to rational agency. This argument was based on his striking doctrine that a rational will must be regarded as autonomous, or free, in the sense of being the author of the law that binds it. The fundamental principle of morality — the CI — is none other than the law of an autonomous will. (from https://plato. stanford.edu/entries/kant-moral/ )

Kant, while recognizing religion's positive influence in society, was interested in creating a moral system without depending upon religion. However, since Kant's stated goal was to save the religiously moral concept of self-sacrifice (perhaps saving it from the burgeoning 18th Century philosophies of reason and rational self-interest from thinkers such as John Locke, Adam Smith, and Edmund Burke), he separated common reason, which was akin to mathematical knowledge, from sensuous knowledge. He suggested that common senses were not sufficient to understand the world. So, how was the world to be understood? Kant posited a higher reality, a higher realm of "knowledge" (echoing Plato's idea of the Ideal Forms). However, since our five senses cannot understand that higher realm, there must be a sixth sense that can. The details of the sense cannot be described since it is assumed rather than clinically studied, but the idea of both personal revelations and personal feelings tend to be candidates for the title. And once you believe that you know the higher realm, what do you do with that knowledge?

Since God's revelations are not mere mundane knowledge but moral laws, Kant therefore favored citizens having moral duties (thus reflecting Rousseau).

Note that both Rousseau and Kant had doubts about "pure reason", i.e. the rational faculty, but they had no doubts about the individual's "duty" to society.

Conversely, the third party in this unintended alliance, which I suggest influenced the formation Post-modernism, certainly supported reason. Surprisingly, this was Albert Einstein. No, Einstein did not publish books on philosophy or religion, but his theories of Relativity changed the understanding of nature, of the universe, and thus of reality itself. Many in my generation grew up mindlessly repeating the bywords of the day: "Everything is relative." Einstein quite rationally proved that a person's perception is relative to his position in space as well as his movement. Thus he proved that things were not always as they first appeared.

If we look at a pencil in a glass of water, it may appear broken, but that is because the water bends the light waves that allow us to see the pencil. Take the pencil out of the water, and we can confirm that it is not broken because the light waves can function without deflection. The revelation of Relativity cast doubt upon *appearances*, not rationality, since clearly one can confirm the solidity of the pencil with a rational approach—by using one's other senses. However, the common citizen did not fully understand Einstein's ideas and they often were content simply to bring into lasting popularity a partial understanding of one of them: "everything is relative".

To summarize a complicated and nuanced philosophical history: distrust of reason (Rousseau), a separate reality (Kant), and everything being relative (Einstein) joined, in my opinion, to give Derrida, Foucault, et al. the fundamental recurring concepts of Postmodernism as outlined below:

| | |
|---|---|
| Social Constructivism | Meaning, morality, and truth do not exist objectively. They are constructed by society |
| Cultural Determinism | Individuals are shaped by cultural forces. Language in particular determines what we can think, trapping us in a "prison house of language" |
| The Rejection of Individual Identity | People exist primarily as members of groups. Identity is primarily collective. |
| Rejection of Humanism | Values that emphasize the creativity, autonomy, and priority of human beings are misplaced. There is no universal humanity since every culture constitutes its own reality. Groups must empower themselves to assert their own values and to take their placer with other planetary species. |

(continued)

| | |
|---|---|
| The Denial of the Transcendent | There are no absolutes. Even if there were, we would have no access to them since we are bound to our culture and imprisoned in our language. |
| Power Reductionism | All institutions, human relationships, moral values, and human creations are expressions and masks of the primal will to power. |
| The Rejection of Reason | Reason and the impulse to objectify truth are illusory masks for cultural power. |
| Revolutionary Critique of the Existing Order | Modern society with its rationalism, order, and unitary view of truth needs to be replaced by a new world order. The old order must be put away to be replaced by a new, as yet unclearly defined, mode of communal existence. |

Screenshot

[from https://quizlet.com/6266751/8-tenets-of-postmodernism-flash-cards/]

If you have difficulty remembering all these positions, try a shorter version:

• There are multiple interpretations of anything, so there is no underlying objective reality;

• Language is a product of society and it determines what we think;

• There is no individual identity; there is only identity as a member of a group; and

• All relationships are power-relationships (victim vs. oppressor) between groups.

Post-modernism was influencing academia well before I was beginning to buy audio courses. The "relativism" of Tony Robbins's Unlimited Power came later than, and was a far cry from, the relativism of Postmodernism. But the most important difference is not where or when Neuro-lingusitic relativism occurred. The most important difference is that Neuro-linguistic Programming (NLP) gives tools with which a person can improve his/her own life while Postmodernism gives beliefs that attempt to reprogram entire cultures and societies. NLP is adopted by personal choice. Postmodernism is more insidious because, although it cannot be adopted except by personal choice, once adopted, it tends to gradually influence all aspects of societies, smuggling in the no-reality concept under the guise of individual thinking.

Why do people in the world today (circa 2023) prefer winning to knowing the truth? Corruption in every field of endeavor (government, art, medicine, law, etc.) produces "winners" that never should have won if there had been objective standards and there had been no verbal-philosophical shenanigans affecting the processes by which people function. We are corrupt to the extent that we do not hold high standards. We let our standards slip to the extent that we can convince ourselves we are doing something good when we may be actually doing something with which we would not want to be associated.

The result is that people no longer want to work toward success, rather they prefer to seize success the easiest way possible, even if it means undercutting those who deserve it. How has this occurred? How can it increasingly occur? One of the prime contributors, mastered by the Post-modernists, is the contorted use of language.

Most people are not astute in understanding the details of their own language, thus they satisfy themselves with enough understanding to get along with people with whom they work and with whom they interact. Advertising and popular songs tend to use the current common vernacular in order to relate to the potential customer or audience and therefore that customer has less incentive to understand what words literally mean or how they can be distorted. Decades ago, I read a statistic that shocked me: 5% of Americans buy 95% of the books, and 90% of those books are not read completely. Have things improved in the twenty-first century?

We occasionally read something on the Internet, and often write messages or emails to each other (rather than call), but the vast majority of what we read are short paragraphs or graphic memes on social media sites, and our writing is too often in abbreviated texts, TY VM!

Once someone presents a concept in a social or political movement, he/she takes pains to name it in a way that will sound attractive to others, but the adherents to that movement never take pains to determine how the concept, if put into practice, might psychologically or socially affect people or their culture. As a result, those who wish to manipulate the mind do so subtly with familiar words intended to avert the listener from fully understanding the concepts that those words allegedly represent.

The remainder of this book is comprised of short chapters on several of those words or phrases. Whether or not you agree with my analysis of the common interpretations and misinterpretation of my specific choices, please consider the wider concept—that in order to support something, you must understand it—really understand it, not simply feel that it sounds good and probably means what you want it to mean. If you do not take the time to really understand, you will easily fall prey to deceivers and, unfortunately, end up living a lie you had never intended to live.

**A man who deliberately inflicts violence on the language will almost certainly inflict violence on human beings if he acquires the power. Those who treasure the meaning of words will treasure truth, and those who bend words to their [own] purposes are very likely in pursuit of anti-social ones. The correct and honorable use of words is the first and natural credential of civilized status.**
**—Paul Johnson, *Enemies of Society***

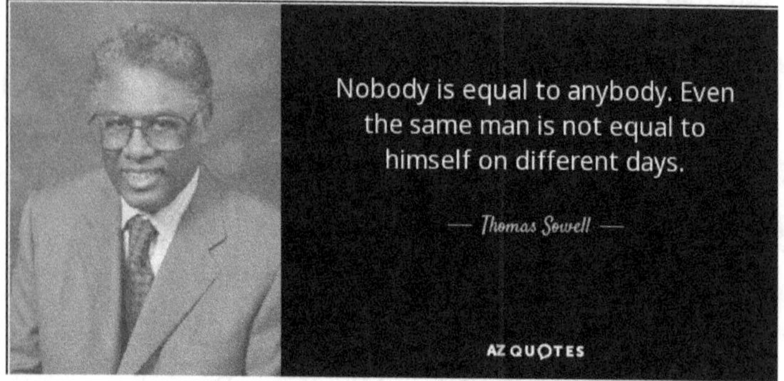

Nobody is equal to anybody. Even the same man is not equal to himself on different days.
— Thomas Sowell —
AZ QUOTES

# 1. Equity ≠ Equality
# Equality ≠ Identity

Equity, in its current use, suggests sameness of result. Equality is more variable, but in contemporary society, it generally refers to equal treatment under the law. The fact that we use the terms equal and equality to refer to several different situations obfuscates the meanings of the terms.

In the math formula $2 + 1 = 3$, the implication of "equals" is that the items on one side of the equation are the same as the items on the other side of the equation. For calculation purposes, then, this is equity. However, a moment's glance will reveal that the left side of the equation has two items while the right side has only one. This makes for an equity that is unequal, that is, if "equal" means identical. To complicate matters, what if we gave a similar but different formula such as $1 + 2 = 3$? Is it equitable to $2 + 1 = 3$? The results are the same but the digits on the left side of the equation do not appear in the same order. What is an equality-minded, socially active, moralistic crusader to do? Perhaps math is inherently biased!

**But, dear author, it is not that simple! One plus one does not always equal two. Sometimes it equals one and sometimes it equals three. If you take two separate puddles of water and put them together you have only one puddle. So one and one equals one. If you take one man and one woman and you put them in a domicile, in nine months you may have three. So one and one equals three.**

Very clever. And either dishonest or unintentionally ignorant of the idea of mixing apples and oranges. With the puddles, you want to count the objects, however the addition comes by measuring the volume of the liquid. Two puddles together equals twice as much liquid albeit in one "container". A man and a woman mating produces a third human being—the objects you wish to count—but that simplistic equation ignores the chemical reactions and nutritional additions that must occur to form the new child. If you have an apple and an orange and add them together, they will still equal one apple and one orange, but they will nevertheless be two fruits.

The problem with equality of results (equity) is that it is illusive unless we are doing math and are interested in sums and products in a very limited way. In the world in which we live, no one is really equal to anyone else. Everyone is both physically and mentally different from everyone else. If we were robots made at the same time, perhaps functional equality would be attainable, but that would eliminate the richness of diversity, which those who strive for social equity also desire.

**But, dear author, what about identical twins? They are both human and also equal.**

Nope. Sorry. One of them is minutes older than the other. Fraternal twins are obviously different looking. In about 21% of even identical twins, one is right-handed, the other left-handed. Identical twins can also be different heights. Their hairline parts can be non-identical. These things are true before adding the complicating factor of subtle differences in nurturing. All of that means that twins can be as *equal* as possible without being perfectly *identical*.

When people talk about social equity, they usually are saying that certain people (usually delineated by an identity-group) are not treated as well as other people (also delineated by an identity-group). Note that identity may be what you think you are, but it does not hold the meaning of its adjectival form "identical". So the activists want equal results for all things unequal while maintain diversity without diverse results.

**But, dear author, equity doesn't have to mean identical earnings or identical social standing. Rather, it should be understood as improved income and social standing so that certain groups are no longer underclasses.**

Thanks for the clarification. If those underclasses improved, but were still comparatively earning less than others, would you still consider it equity? I don't think so.

It would be wonderful to see a society in which people could constantly improve their incomes without worrying about the complaints of someone else who is unable or unwilling to improve his/her income. How would we do that? By constantly redistributing income? By having a national income that could not be exceeded? In that case, why would people take care to make careful decisions about their goals, their work, or their investments? What incentive would people have to work hard rather than do as little as possible? In my opinion, equity is an unrealistic, unworkable goal. I would prefer a society in which all people, regardless of their income or social status, could live comfortably and provide for themselves. The government should be there not to artificially make the results of all efforts equitable, but to safeguard fair play so that the rich do not deceive the poor or so that the poor do not willingly put themselves into deeper poverty so that they will qualify to live off the state.

In the USA, and indeed in the world, poverty is constantly going down, but income disparities constantly go up. I agree with the idea of equality giving the opportunity for constant growth, but not in the idea of demanding that the end result being necessarily closer than it is, let alone being the same.

Another meaning of equity is "the value of shares in a company". Would social activists want all stocks to have the same equity or would they want all investors to earn (or lose) the same amount regardless of their stock choices? Equity is not only impossible but also undesirable. Fair and equal treatment in society can also be elusive, but it is much more attainable.

Equity (sameness of results) implies that everyone will share the same identity, but aren't the devotees of equity also the fans of every person imagining their own personal identity?

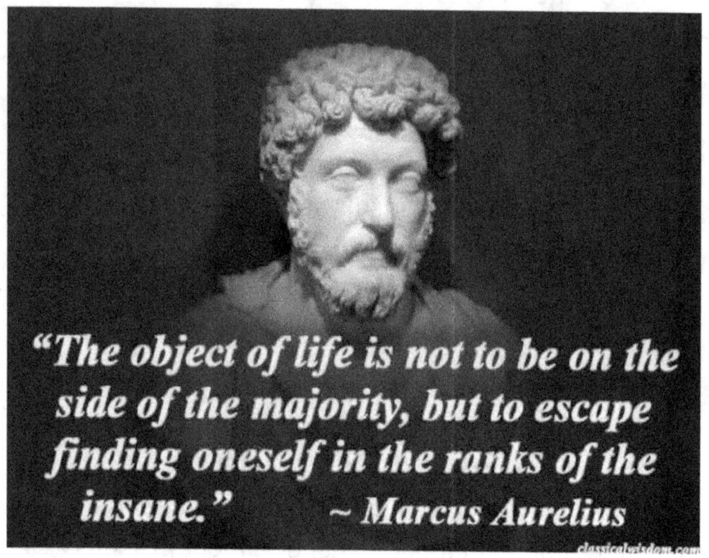
"The object of life is not to be on the side of the majority, but to escape finding oneself in the ranks of the insane."
~ Marcus Aurelius
classicalwisdom.com

# 2. Self-identity ≠ Actual Identity

If everyone cannot be the same or have the same results in the things that they work for, invest in, or study, then perhaps equity should step aside and make room for personal identity. Yet, those who advocate social equity seem to look down upon traditional American individualism, but still manage to embrace self-identity. That is to say, some believe that whatever one fervently wishes to be *actually* is what one is, as if their mind was so powerful that it could change objective reality with a wish. Yet, to many of these people, when someone else wants to follow his/own stars, he/she must be advocating a rugged individualism that is somehow dangerous to society since it does not consider others as a primary (since, of course, the wellbeing of others is more important than one's personal self-expression). If this seems confusing, that's because anything that is self-contradictory usually is. Ironically, those who consider others more important than themselves have reinterpreted Christian ethics while simultaneously expressing a dislike for Christian ethics. Those who consider others (or the group) more important than the individual still manage to declare their independence through a unique self-identity.

**But, dear author, it is only fair to reverse the concept: those who support rugged individualism (striving to succeed dominantly by one's own efforts) no doubt believe that those who personally identify as something they are not now, or were not born as, are advocating a self-delusion that is dangerous to society—a society on which the individual depends for his/her freedom to act whichever way he/she wishes.**

That is a generally accurate perception, thus a fair objection to consider. However, I would not concur that those who think that identifying oneself as a person of a different gender, for example, is necessarily dangerous to society. What is dangerous to society is that those people expect their personal delusions to be readily accepted by a society that does not share them.

When I was a boy, I walked into one of the town banks to make a deposit and saw a man with hairy legs, a mustache, and lipstick in a skirt and heels standing at the clerk counter in front of me. No one in the building said a word. He completed his transaction and left. No one mocked him and no one called the cops. But it was clear to me that everyone was shocked and would rest easier once he was gone. The wider group was tolerant but uncomfortable. The cross-dressing individual obviously had appeared in public to get a reaction, got it, and then went on his way. (For more on the individual and the group, see my book *Life is About Control*.) There is an important difference between tolerance and acceptance. In today's world we are supposed to accept not simply cross-dressing, but cross-identifying, even when a person does not go through the hormone therapy and surgeries to make the transition thorough enough so that it is not simply a stunt for attention.

We need not debate about people's freedom to see themselves in any way they prefer, whether we think it realistic or not. People are free to think any way they wish. Nevertheless, to many people, a man who "identifies" as a woman is more absurd than calling a politician a statesman, or calling a fungus a pet. In most Western societies, a biological woman who prefers to be a male can indulge or act on her preferences and a biological male is free to indulge his fantasies of experiencing womanhood despite his XY chromosomes. This sort of preference is therefore no business of those people who may find it absurd. If he/she decides to invest in hormone therapy and surgery to fulfill his/her desires to change gender, that is no business of anyone except the person and his/her doctors.

However, this sort of circumstance provides the prospect of a debate, or at least a discussion, from an intellectual perspective. If his self-identity equalled his *actual* identity, he would not *have* to endure any therapy or surgery at all. Although his mental disposition may lead him to take physical action that adjusts his appearance, the mental disposition itself does not complete the transition. Wanting something and believing that because of the want the *fact* already exists is an exercise in thought twisting.

**But, dear author, a person, I'm sure you would agree, has the right to act in any way he or she wants that does not cause harm to others!**

The social furor over gender reassignment is not about the rights of adult citizens, nor about other people's attitude toward a person exercising his/her rights; rather, the furor arrises when one of three things occur:

(1) when a transgender (or non-binary) person demands social acceptance for his/her preferred identity or identities,

(2) when a transgender (or non-binary) person is hired or appointed to position because of his/her unconventional identity choices, and

(3) when transgenders (or non-binaries) attempt

to convince children that they should make gender affirming or denying decisions before they are adults, and in some cases, before they even reach puberty.

**As regards (1) social acceptance.** People in societies tend to congregate with like-minded people, automatically ignoring those who are not like-minded. Therefore, although a person who displays aberrant behavior is free to do so (if it does not conflict with the rights of others), that person has no right to demand that people think of him/her a certain way. A person's uniqueness of thought regarding self-identity does not imply that others should give up their own uniqueness of thought.

**As regards (2) preferential treatment.** Your accepting a position because the person who appointed or hired you wants to show off his/her tolerance and support for your behavior is like accepting a lottery payoff that someone else's ticket won, just so the store in which it was purchased can share a portion of the wealth. You did not choose the number or buy the ticket, but you are happy to abscond with the funds, and you are supported in doing so by those who want to benefit from your claim since unclaimed tickets, depending on the locale, may not benefit anyone.

More importantly, if the transgender person is unqualified for the position, the possibility of harming others via his/her incompetence comes into play, so preferential treatment is actually a preference for image over success.

**As regards (3) converting children.** The primary concern is in the practice of foisting any subject or practice upon those under the legal age of consent. If any action has to be kept from parents of the targeted children, that action is suspect. Whether the secret subject is a revisionist take on history, a social cause, or a personal behavior, if it is not previously within the approved school curriculum and also sanctioned by parents, it should not be taught, exhibited, or encouraged.

**But, dear author, schools cannot run every curriculum and every extra-curricular activity past the parents. To do so would mean weekly parent-teacher meetings and a lot of catering to parents who know nothing about educational methods.**

True, but parents can insist on *a committee of parents* to approve the initial curricula and any changes during the year. Parents may not be professional teachers, but that does not mean that they know nothing about what is best for their own children or about education in general, twelve years of which most parents survived.

Why would a person who has made a personal decision that is extremely out of the mainstream of the culture, like gender-reassignment or drag-queen behavior, wish to influence the most impressionable in the culture, despite what parents may think? One may as well ask why people seem to want to be among like-minded folks. I would contend that the thought process of the gender benders is as follows: If the parents of these children do not accept us, perhaps the children will. If so, perhaps the future culture will be influenced so that such "personal gender decisions" will not seem out of the mainstream. It's not that misery loves company; it is that people, having decided to be different (perhaps courageously, considering the dominant preferences of their culture), cannot hold on to that courage continually. They thus maintain a separate sub-culture. This desire to be "mainstreamed" by pulling the sub-culture into the dominant culture, unfortunately takes the step of emotionally harming others by confusing developing minds and sexualizing life before those minds have even asked about sexuality. The gender identity advocates do this in order to avoid the chance of being emotionally "harmed" themselves—by exclusion.

I know two people who have changed their genders. Neither makes a big deal about it. Once the transition was made, they changed their names but went on with their professions, sufficiently assured in their decisions so that they did not need to convert others to their points of view.

If an adult's personal choice does not harm anyone else, it should remain free, however the idea of "harming anyone else" is subject to definition and debate. Most people are uncomfortable with the unconventional personal decisions of others precisely because they fear that those decisions, if not directly harmful, will begin to infiltrate the culture and gradually be accepted as normal or conventional—two other terms that are subject to both definition and debate. The aberrant group wants to be mainstreamed while the tolerant but uninterested group wants the aberrant to remain as a subculture.

When is a choice dangerous to others? When is social deviance tolerable and when is it equivalent to insane (thus intolerable) behavior? I discuss this in *Life is About Control*, a section of which I quote here:

Normally functioning citizens release the tension of everyday self-control through many methods that are tolerated, understood, and sometimes even encouraged in a civilized society. Among these are becoming intoxicated or high, attempting a risky physical activity, taking a day of total pampering, taking a vacation, making crazy love, experiencing a sensory deprivation chamber, resting with earphones playing your favorite music, bingeing a favorite TV show, etc. In essence, these are tools that help retain one's self-control because they are applied when the usual concentrated effort of self-control or hard work becomes taxing and thus inefficient. None of these activities are considered mentally ill. Although they may sometimes put your rational faculties on pause, they are not irrational because they do not hurt you or others if done with normal intensity and duration. However, if people engage in either a self-destructive or an other-destructive activity to make themselves feel more alive, virtuous, or worthwhile, I would suggest considering that a mental illness may exist—either an individual or a collective psychosis.

The extreme self-identity movement, the principals of which not only are unhappy with the self that nature produced, but also expect everyone else to participate, without even flinching, in their personal preferred selves, may also trace its roots to the self-development trends of earlier decades.

I remember first encountering the sales-oriented phrase, "If it is to be, it's up to me", and understood it to be a reasonable nudge toward self-motivation. Later, I discovered "Fake it until you make it." I didn't like faking anything, but I could accept this admonition as a little trick one could play within one's own mind. You would *pretend* to be successful at your endeavor in order to adopt the characteristics that would *make* you successful in that endeavor. This "fake it" concept interfaced with people's tendency to judge a person by external appearances or trivial actions before they actually came to know the person. Salesmen were encouraged to arrive at their appointments in a washed, waxed, and if possible, shiny new and expensive car in order to look successful. My lawyer kept her old Mercedes because the new Toyota that would have been more economic for her traveling purposes did not convey the idea of "success" to her clients. (Indeed, many politicians invest more on looking good to the public or looking like they care about constituents than they invest in actually addressing problems. To them, appearances are everything.) Even more pertinent to the self-development concept is the fact that success coaches have encouraged us to imagine our present ourselves the way we want our future selves to be.

I would not deny the validity of "faking it until you make it" as a way of programming your own brain for success so long as you don't fake yourself out of money or safety in hopes that your jackpot of riches is right around the proverbial corner. I knew a couple who wanted an expensive recreational vehicle for vacationing, but they were fledglings in their new business. Following the "fake it" self-development advice, they bought the RV, but their business did not grow as expected. After two vacations, they were obliged to sell the RV that they had always wanted. Was the self-development advice unsound? Or, were they taking it too literally and thus not applying common sense to its timing and execution?

If self-identity equaled actual identity, that couple would not have to be successful in their business. Their simply identifying as RV-owners would have made their wish a reality. Self-identity can avoid self-delusion only if one measures one's changing identity in terms of objective reality. Business-owners may image themselves as very successful with 47-branch stores and an annual income of $14 million, but before that goal is reached, they must have several successful years in one really successful store and then satisfy themselves with reinvesting the lion's share of their income to open and stock the second store. Change seldom happens overnight. Even gender-reassignment requires more than a few "overnights" of hormone therapy, lifestyle adaptation, and recovery from whatever physical modifications have been made surgically.

**But, dear author, its not that people who identify as something they are not (at present), but sincerely want to be, need to convince others to join or accept them. It is that their very difference means that others will not treat them equally and often will exhibit discriminatory practices when dealing with them.**

I suggest that you want people to believe that not accepting a practice is the same as discriminating against the person. Not necessarily….

"Many issues are misconstrued, not because they are too complex for most people to understand, but because a mundane explanation is far less emotionally satisfying than an explanation which produces villains to hate and heroes to exalt."

*Thomas Sowell*

t.me/ThomasSowellQuote

# 3. Disparities ≠ Discrimination

In his *Discrimination and Disparities*, Thomas Sowell explains that in most cases the statistical difference we see between Whites and Blacks in the USA may exist for several reasons other than racial bias. His thesis helps link this book's Chapter 1. *Equity ≠ Equality / Equality ≠ Identity* with Chapter 2. *Self-identity ≠ Actual Identity*.

The idea that Disparities do not necessarily suggest any sort of Discrimination applies to all choices and actions, not simply to racial situations.

If your team loses a basketball game, that loss does not imply that the other team cheated or that the referees were incompetent. It is more likely to imply that the winner was better, or that your team was not at its best in that specific contest.

When you do not get a job, it may be because you didn't shower that day or because the tattoo on your face would not seem welcoming when interfacing with potential customers, but is your lack of employment due to the hiring agent's bias for pleasant smelling, un-decorated skin? Well, yes and no. The hiring agent did have a bias, but it was a logical, understandable bias. If you are a nudist, you do not show up to job interviews naked. The interviewer might really like your body, but it is unlikely she will want you to represent a business that interacts with customers who preferred to make their transactions while fully clothed.

If you are not accepted into a university because your SAT scores are in the 400s, is it really because you are Black, Lesbian, or Lithuanian? If you *were* accepted because you are Black, Lesbian, or Lithuanian *despite* your SAT scores in the 400s, wouldn't that be discrimi-nation? After all, the non-Black, non-Lesbian, and non-Lithuanian applicants were all expected to have SAT scores in the 600s.

Frankly, almost nobody cares what you identify as. Rather, they care that you don't throw it in their faces, ask them to recognize your preference as if they did not see it otherwise, or take advantage of a sometimes influential minority that wants you to be comfortable and will sacrifice the wellbeing of the majority to publicly prove it. Few people truly want to be discriminatory regarding the idiosyncrasies of others. In most relatively free countries, you don't have to conform, but you have to accept that convention may not embrace your idiosyncrasy as a standard for humanity.

Self-identification is a personal thing that takes a few seconds of mental energy. However, accepting anyone else's self-identification is a constant battle of trying to beat back the reality one has gradually come to know and depend upon.

Not only does objective reality tend to conflict with some personal self-perspectives, but the average person has his hands (and mind) full just trying to understand objective reality itself, and the social activities that may be based on a specific view of reality.

The average person must depend on educated, credentialed, informed intellects in his culture to inform him. Unfortunately, sometimes those intellects are less than rational.

"Much of the social history of the Western world over the past three decades has involved replacing what worked with what sounded good. In area after area – crime, education, housing, race relations – the situation has gotten worse after the bright new theories were put into operation."

~Thomas Sowell
1993-  "Is Reality Optional"

# 4. Intelligence ≠ Rationality<br>Expertise ≠ Accuracy

Since we cannot know everything, we look for those that teach, write articles, books, or blogs, offer online videos, etc. to inform us. We tend to believe two kinds of people: those who sound like they have adopted the opinion we already hold (but for which we seek more authoritative confirmation) and those with more experience, many of which we believe are "experts". (The word *expert* comes from the Latin *expertus* and is related to both *experience* and *experiment*.)

Clearly experts have become known as experts because they are knowledgable about certain fields of study. Many of them, like college professors, earned advanced degrees in those fields. Some of them, like department heads in business and government, have been given positions of responsibility within those fields. They know far more than we do about their fields of expertise, so if we are going to believe someone, it might as well be the alleged expert.

Unfortunately, not only do experts disagree with each other within their fields, but also they tend to parley their knowledge in one field as a generic kind of expertise in fields unrelated to their own. Because of their knowledge in one field, we are supposed to believe that they must be accurate, dependable, and even irrefutable in other fields. After all, the discipline and detailed precision it took to achieve in one area applies to other areas, don't they?

Experts can be very intelligent generally yet remain unskilled in any field except perhaps the one in which they specialize. They then use their intellects to *sound* reasonable and dependable, knowing they may be able to convince you of the validity of their ideas where another, perhaps more accurate, expert may not have such rhetorical skills. Epidemiologists know about epidemics, but what do they know about public policy? Computer scientists know a lot about computer code and the hardware that handles it, but what do they know about epidemiology?

I would conclude then that intelligence does not necessarily equal expertise and that expertise does not necessarily equal accuracy. Even the most intelligent experts cannot be certain of every idea that occurs in their fields. As mentioned, we would hope that their intelligence and expertise would have given them sufficient practice in careful, critical thinking so that their investigations in their fields would proceed rationally, i.e. with sufficient attention to reason and logic. Further, we would hope that their public statements about ideas in their fields could be defended with reason and logic, not with a carefully worded caricature of reason and logic intended to sound erudite while playing upon fundamental emotions.

Why do we *not* recognize when an expert is playing word games rather than expounding factually on his/her discoveries? I suspect it is because many decades of product advertising, especially on TV, has inured us to arguments that avoid careful logic and habituated us to make instant, often emotional, decisions.

Advertisers have investigated what encourages the maximum number people to purchase an item most of the time. They present you with a familiar problem, give you a potential solution, make you trust them by using your favorite sports or movie stars as spokespersons, convince you with user endorsements, present you with a call to action and often a deadline, and then repeat their phone number three times. Somewhere hidden in the commercial is 5.3 seconds about scientific tests or statistical measurements. Other than that, it is a fast paced, emotion-stimulating sequence of convincer strategies.

It seems to me that over my lifetime, experts that once took responsibility for explaining difficult concepts to the lay person, in universities, in books, and in media, now either write and speak for a closed house of other experts or use their expertise to satisfy a hidden lust for fame. In the latter case, truth sometimes takes a back seat to celebrity.

In the past, experts were known for their ability to predict a certain outcome based on their vast experience in their field. That, in fact, is how science works: a theory first seems reasonable, but rises from the merely possible to the status of fact when the theory regularly predicts outcomes. In the last century, Relativity, Continental Drift, and The Big Bang origin of the universe were all severely doubted until further evidence proved them to be true. Currently however, both our society and its experts, it seems, have become too impatient for empirical confirmation. Instead, the experts offer, and the society accepts, not predictions that can be tested, but conclusions that allegedly need not be tested, as if they had already risen to the level of fact.

I remember all the "experts" warning the population of the earth about the imminent technological crash of Y2K. Our devices were not pre-programmed for dates beyond 2000, so no doubt planes would fall from the sky when their computers no longer worked.

Paul Ehrlich, an expert on population and ecology from Stanford University and co-author of *The Population Bomb*, had these predictions—and these results:

...In 1964, he said that the Indian vasectomy program was going to fail because of the beliefs of the populace and technical problems. The program is not an entire failure.

--In 1969, he claimed that it was "ignorant and irresponsible" to expect increased food production from underwater farming. In 1970, food production increased in Asia because of marine agriculture.

--In 1972, he said that 1973 smog disasters in Los Angeles and New York would leave 200,000 dead. He painted a picture of hundreds of people dying without medical help in hospitals, while others watched on their television screens. It would be announced, he said, that Americans born since 1946 (when DDT came into wide use) had a life expectancy of 49 years. Neither event has happened, though smog and DDT remain real dangers.

...In 1972, he predicted that water rationing would occur in nearly 2,000 municipalities in 1974 and that hepatitis and epidemic dysentery rates would go up 500%. Neither event took place.

--In 1972, he said that, because of a shift of the jet stream caused by air pollution, a permanent drought would occur in the Midwest, turning it into a desert. In reaction, the economy would start to fail. This has not happened.

Source: https://www.trivia-library.com/a/past-predictions-by-famous-scientist-dr-paul-ehrlich.htm

William H. Stewart, Surgeon General of the USA, said in 1969 that we could close the books on infectious diseases.

Even an expert as eminent as Albert Einstein said in 1932, "There is not the slightest indication that nuclear energy will ever be attainable."

When we listen to experts or even seemingly intelligent people, how can we discern if their arguments are to be seriously considered? If objective evidence in support of their ideas is not immediately forthcoming, to which aspects of an expert's arguments should we give temporary credence? What would make us think that, yes, maybe this could be true? Don't experts' arguments have to be rational as well as intelligent-sounding or clever? The rational standard of judgment would suggest that we, the listener, must be able to discern logic and reason from wishful thinking and double-talk.

Descending from Aristotle, there are three rules of logic:

(1) The Law of Identity (a thing is what it is and not what it is not),

(2) The Law of Non-contradiction (something cannot be both True and False in the same way at the same time), and

(3) The Law of the Excluded Middle (there is only Truth and Falsity; there is no third option).

You may wish to read them again. I would

wager that you immediately will try to find exceptions to each rule. Good. That is critical thinking. Over millennia intelligent people have attempted to find those exceptions, but in order to do so, they have to subtly or cleverly misinterpret of one of these rules.

**But dear author, don't we always seem to find gray areas in every endeavor? The rule that is vulnerable to an exception is certainly Rule #3, The Excluded Middle.**

Yes, we do find gray areas; but we usually confuse the gray areas of personalities and preferences with the alleged gray areas of logic. Take for example, the congresswoman who is rabidly for strict gun control and defunding the police, but has hired a private security force, guns and all, to protect her. She claims that she is an exception to her anti-gun-anti-police position because she needs the protection from those rabid gun-owners who don't like her. Is she being blatantly illogical? Or is her philosophical inconsistency understandable and acceptable? How about the celebrities who travel to climate conferences on their private jets to rail about $CO_2$ emissions? Each private jet emits more $CO_2$ on one flight than a dozen commercial airliners. Those celebrities are certainly pressed for time, and have to get back to Hollywood for their latest movie shoot, but is their apparent hypocrisy illogical?

**Agree with them or not, it seems harsh to ap-**

ply a standard of non-contradictory action to human beings. A person can say he is on a diet even if he cheats a little on Sundays, can't he?

Right, it does seem harsh, but that harshness does not make inconsistency logical! If it is self-contradictory, it flies in the face of Rule #2, The Law of Non-contradiction.

Even your developing an understanding of logic does not make you immune to verbal shenanigans and clever phraseology! To defend against these, one must understand fallacious verbal reasoning, as well. Below I offer a list of these *(facing page)*.

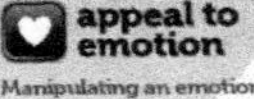

strawman
Misrepresenting or exaggerating someone's argument to make it easier to attack.

slippery slope
Asserting that if we allow A to happen, then Z will consequently happen too, therefore A should not happen.

special pleading
Moving the goalposts or making up exceptions when a claim is shown to be false.

the gambler's fallacy
Believing that 'runs' occur to statistically independent phenomena such as roulette wheel spins.

black-or-white
Where two alternative states are presented as the only possibilities, when in fact more possibilities exist.

false cause
Presuming that a real or perceived relationship between things means that one is the cause of the other.

ad hominem
Attacking your opponent's character or personal traits instead of engaging with their argument.

loaded question
Asking a question that has an assumption built into it so that it can't be answered without appearing guilty.

bandwagon
Appealing to popularity or the fact that many people do something as an attempted form of validation.

begging the question
A circular argument in which the conclusion is included in the premise.

appeal to authority
Using the opinion or position of an authority figure, or institution of authority, in place of an actual argument.

appeal to nature
Making the argument that because something is 'natural' it is therefore valid, justified, inevitable, or ideal.

composition /division
Assuming that what's true about one part of something has to be applied to all, or other, parts of it.

anecdotal
Using personal experience or an isolated example instead of a valid argument, especially to dismiss statistics.

appeal to emotion
Manipulating an emotional response in place of a valid or compelling argument.

tu quoque
Avoiding having to engage with criticism by turning it back on the accuser - answering them with criticism.

burden of proof
Saying that the burden of proof lies not with the person making the claim, but with someone else to disprove.

no true scotsman
Making what could be called an appeal to purity as a way to dismiss relevant criticisms or flaws of an argument.

the texas sharpshooter
Cherry-picking data clusters to suit an argument, or finding a pattern to fit a presumption.

the fallacy fallacy
Presuming that because a claim has been poorly argued or a fallacy has been made, that it is necessarily wrong.

personal incredulity
Saying that because one finds something difficult to understand that it's therefore not true.

ambiguity
Using double meanings or ambiguities of language to mislead or misrepresent the truth.

genetic
Judging something good or bad on the basis of where it comes from, or from whom it comes.

middle ground
Saying that a compromise, or middle point, between two extremes is the truth.

thou shalt not commit logical fallacies

Knowing the above fallacies will help enormously, yet there are still cunning ways in which word wizardry can catch even the most intelligent person unaware. What if Mr. Econ O'Politicus offered his new economic plan as one that will enhance the solvency of the masses? It sounds good until one realizes that all economic philosophies, systems, and plans are meant to enhance the solvency of the masses. Regardless of their real world record, all economic methods (whether leaning toward Capitalism, Fascism, or Socialism) are intended to make goods and services available as widely and as efficiently as possible. If we had no such methods, we would simply barter locally to create and distribute goods. Bartering is an old and inefficient economic system, but still an economic system. This kind of irony (making a generality sound exclusive) may fall under the fallacy of "Strawman", "Begging the Question", "Ambiguity", or even "Appeal to Emotion", but because it is not easily pinned to a specific logical fallacy, we tend to let it slip our awareness.

We need to discern truth from falsehood in order to know whether to trust "experts"; but also, we want to be right in order to feel emotionally satisfied and competent to survive in a confusing world. Wanting to be right sets the stage for accepting an intellectual position that satisfies us emotionally. Therein lies a hidden but very threatening danger. Tom Nichols in his *The Death of Expertise* writes *[the word in brackets is mine]*:

> When feelings matter more that rationality or facts, education is a doomed enterprise. Emotion is an unassailable defense against [true] expertise, a moat of anger and resentment in which reason and knowledge quickly drown. And when students learn that emotion trumps everything else, it is a lesson they will take with them for the rest of their lives.

"The human being cannot live in a condition of emptiness for very long: if he is not growing toward something, he does not merely stagnate; the pent-up potentialities turn into morbidity and despair, and eventually into destructive activities."

— Rollo May

# 5. Riots ≠ Demonstrations Mob Rule ≠ Democracy

The only thing we seem to want more than to be correct is to be ethical. Perhaps it is more accurate to say that we want to *feel* ethically superior or at least ethically *justified*. To feel ethically justified, we must perform some act that would seem unethical in usual circumstances, but tell ourselves that it was morally defensible. To feel ethically superior, we must have an opponent, a contender, or an enemy who is ethically inferior. A social cause provides both an ethically inferior bad-guy and a way to exercise an injustice while appearing to be a warrior for elusive social or economic justice (always for the good of others, of course).

When people feel their rights have been infringed, but the government that we have elected to protect those rights seems not to care, they will raise its attention, and the attention of like-minded people, by staging a demonstration. Demonstrations are meant to legally interrupt the normal operating procedure of society, otherwise they could not garner attention. The organizers of marches either for a cause or against a policy obtain a city's permission to use a specific locale or route so that the demonstrators will not be arrested for disturbing the peace. What if they do disturb the peace? What if they do not obtain permission to demonstrate? Isn't that what Henry David Thoreau termed "civil disobedience"—a much vaunted American tradition that has been used ever since 1849 to support ignored causes? Maybe. Do the civilly disobedient expect to be arrested and to pay their fines or willingly suffer other penalties? Or do they expect to disturb the peace, appear on their favorite cable news network, and then stroll home un-arrested or at least un-incarcerated? Civil disobedience means that the disobedient will endure the penalty of his/her actions in order to make a point. Today, the disobedient hide behind the rubric of "civil disobedience" and "social justice" when they want to destroy and want to feel justified in doing so. Henry David Thoreau writes in his Civil Disobedience, "What I have to do is to see, at any rate, that I do not lend myself to the wrong which I condemn."

At the risk of repeating my favorite memes (the following was used in my previous book *Life Is About Control*), here is John Cleese on "political extremism":

Too often, demonstrations are either infiltrated by an undisciplined element who become destructive, or they are intended to morph first into a disturbance and then, when not contained by police, a manifestation of mayhem, as if mob rule were a regularly acceptable expression of discontent.

Since everyone in a mob cooperates in the mob action, some people actually believe that the mob is an expression of democratic will. When one is taken up by such a deluge, it is hardly an expression of simply contributing toward proper irrigation. Even if one votes for the destructive mob action, the democracy one exhibits is a very limited sort of democracy—one that illustrates why the Founding Fathers of the USA preferred a constitutional republic to a direct democracy.

One may argue that democracy is the rightful expression of the will of the people! It is an expression of the will of the majority, but it should not be used to ignore the rights of the minority, as we will discuss in the following chapter.

Today, however, people use the idea of "democracy" to justify their actions, just as they use the idea of demonstrations to justify their riots. What they want is not the will of the people; what they want is simply to have their own way. Why is it that people now prefer winning to the truth or to the legitimate will of the people? The short answer is corruption. If the people feel they no longer trust their institutions, they will act riotously, call it democracy, all the while believing that they are morally correct and thus justified in their show of illegal force. The only difference between them and corrupt public actors is that corrupt actors know they are corrupt and only *pretend* to be acting "for the people". Sincerely convinced (even if incorrect) actors believe they are both correct and moral. To them, excessive use of force is not illegal, but is the understandable reaction of disenfranchised citizens. Because they cannot (or choose not to) reason carefully and separate cold fact from hot fantasy, they see themselves as free people exercising their "democratic" freedoms (as will be discussed in Chapter 7).

Power is not controlling other people. Power is controlling yourself. Trying to control other people is the first sign that you are entirely out of control. Controlling others is what weak people think power looks like.

-Kalen Dion-

# 6. A Democracy ≠ A Republic

Also from *Civil Disobedience*: "The government itself, which is only the mode which the people have chosen to execute their will, is equally liable to be abused and perverted before the people can act through it."

Too often, talking heads on TV refer to constitutional republics as "democracies" simply because citizens vote democratically on election day. However, we vote for local and national representatives, who themselves vote for or against laws. The only office for which we truly seem to vote democratically is President of the United States; however, that democratic vote is tempered by one of the famed checks and balances of the US Government—the electoral college system. Electoral votes are meant to protect the less populated states from being dominated by the concentrated votes of the more populated states which are themselves dominated by their very populated cities.

Why didn't the founders, in breaking away from King George III's rule, opt for a straight vote of the people for each important national office? One of the features of the U.S. Constitution is that it recognizes individual rights—rights that allegedly cannot be voted away.

The first ten amendments of the U.S. Constitution make explicit some of these rights. The founders debated over whether the "Bill of Rights" (Amendments 1 through 10) should be enumerated in print. The argument was that if they were enumerated, people would think that there were not more than 10 individual rights; but, if they were not enumerated, people might not recognize that the constitution was meant to limit government overreach, thus recognize *at least* these 10 rights. Obviously, the enumerators won out. And yet, I suspect that people today understand the Bill of Rights as granting them rights rather than limiting the government from taking them away.

Without God-given or natural rights, people would only have privileges as conferred by their government, which would mean that the government could play favorites by legally voting *democratically* to grant special privileges to some people, or to refuse to honor some individual's privilege or his/her rights. Therefore the constitution protects individuals from the government and from those who might wish to democratically vote to violate constitutional rights—rights that the founders agreed should be inviolate.

The added safeguard of being a Republic, rather than a direct Democracy means that not only can people be free to go about their business without having to be knowledgable about each issue in front of Congress on which they would have to vote in a Democracy, but also their representatives would educate their constituents, at least to some degree, about those issues should their representatives wish to earn their vote again.

This somewhat indirect and slow process allows maximum liberty while still making individual voters indirectly responsible for the choices of their government. Without liberty, it stands to reason, people are ruled, not governed. Without responsibility for electing those who represent them, people's freedom would quickly become license.

In essence, direct Democracy would give the state authorization to act without restraint. That is to say: a democracy *per se* is a method by which to control others. A Constitutional Republic allows people more freedom because it restrains governmental actions. In doing so, it depends on personal responsibility (see my book *Life is About Control*).

If liberty means anything at all, it means the right to tell people what they do not want to hear.

George Orwell
Author

# 7. License ≠ Liberty and Freedom to be Unconventional ≠ A Claim to Normality

License is acting without self-restraint or responsibility. Liberty is freedom to act while being responsible for not violating anyone's else rights.

Free people are free to be unconventional, otherwise freedom and liberty mean very little. But people still live among other people who have their own ideas of what should be considered unconventional. What prevents people from doing socially undesirable things that do not directly violate other people's rights? Usually, it is nothing more than convention and consideration. It is convention and mutual consideration that make a social standard that people dub Normal. While one's freedom can extend up to but not beyond the rights of others, people's sensibilities can be offended quite a bit earlier. In order to maintain social harmony, most people do the things that a culture deems socially undesirable only privately or in closed societies. That way, they can enjoy their own freedom and not conflict with the sense of "normality" held by the majority.

In a free society, people may have differing views of what is publicly acceptable. Some people are disgusted by the fact that you dye you hair purple, shave the left half of your head, pierce your eyebrows, and always wear cargo shorts. But your fashion sense does not interfere with their rights, so you get no complaints from them. If, however, you appeared at the annual Daughters of the American Revolution cotillion in your normal street attire, you might be less tolerated. Would you be escorted out? Although you might have to tolerate a lot of background whispering and contact avoidance, you might be tolerated begrudgingly...or you might be expelled. Now what if you were to arrive topless? Whether you were a man or woman, you would no doubt be escorted out.

Tolerance of any kind has its limits. It is tolerance, not necessarily a right, that is tested when people take their personal freedom to act unconventionally over the edge of liberty and into license. If the majority of people are uncomfortable with public exhibitionism, for example, it is fine to consider them prudes and to argue for a more tolerant attitude; however, when one flaunts one's exhibitionism in order to test the reactions of otherwise tolerant people, one is using one's personal preference as a new norm while trying to make the majority feel like a minority. *How dare they get uptight at my going topless to the cotillion! They are the weird ones! Topless is completely natural and I am not going to put up with their puritanical, priggish, straight-laced conventions!*

But all conventions are puritanical, priggish, straight-laced, or totally unnecessary to someone! And no one would be comfortable if everyone exercised his or her personal whims and foibles publicly at every turn.

Driving southward with a friend in southern France where I had spent the afternoon at a topless beach by the local river, we passed a parked car in which a man and a woman, both topless, were evidently switching drivers but stopped to passionately embrace in front of the vehicle. "*C'est courant dans le sud* [It's common in the south]," my friend laughed. He told me with a smile that he had passed a car last summer on which two people were making love on a blanket draped over their car's hood. He said, not unapprovingly, that he fully expected that in ten years, people would be walking around in the nude. Several decades later, that behavior has not occurred, even in the least uptight region of a decidedly un-puritanical country. Why? I

suspect it is because, even when conventions are mini-
mized, people still want them to exist.

The week before, I was sunning at the local
community pool. The people of the little town had voted
to allow topless bathing for women on the grounds of
equal treatment for women and of becoming less Vic-
torian since this was not England but France, and it
was, after all, nearly a new millennium. I wasn't about
to complain, of course, and relaxed on my towel with
my eyes never fully closed. An especially curvy young
woman and her friends, all topless, were walking toward
the refreshment kiosk that overlooked the pool, five con-
crete steps up, but still part of the fenced pool area, and
still in full view of the swimmers. All the girls donned T-
shirts to order their snacks. Whether they were conform-
ing to the letter of the local law or expressing a common
consideration of others, clearly there existed a socially
recognized limit to a clearly liberal adjustment to what
had once been a more restrictive social custom. Wanting
to take advantage of a newly minted liberty, they did not
want to be licentious and thus the girls hid their assets in
order to spend their money.

I continue on a related topic in Chapter 9 (*Idiosyncratic ≠ Idiotic*, etc.), but since the T-shirted damsels
were spending their Francs while covering other assets,
I'll first offer a brief discussion of wealth.

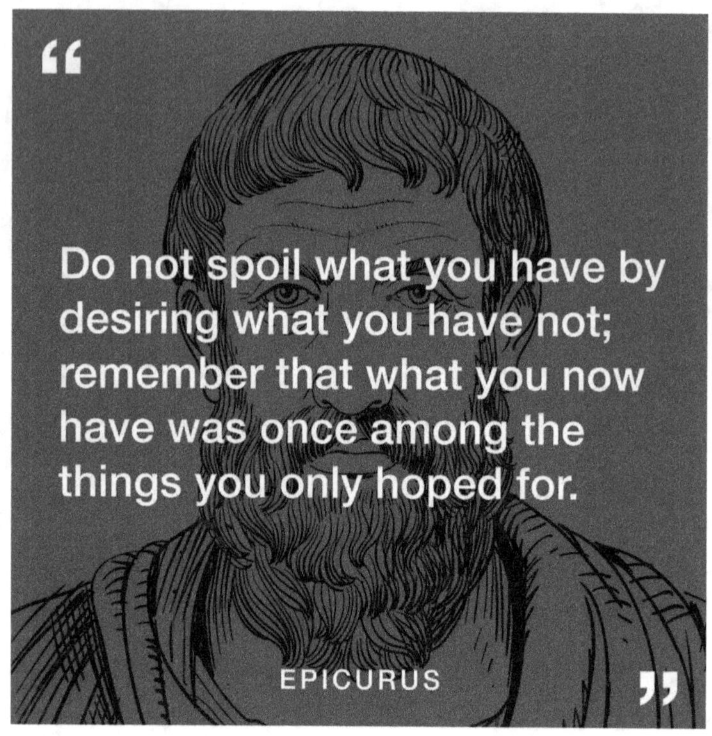
Do not spoil what you have by desiring what you have not; remember that what you now have was once among the things you only hoped for.
EPICURUS

# 8. Money ≠ Wealth

Money is one sort of asset one might possess. A wardrobe, a car, or a home are other sorts of assets. The aggregate of your assets equals your wealth. Even food is an asset until you consume it.

There are also less overt assets such as intelligence, talent, knowledge, and experience. Therefore, you can have a small bank account but be wealthy in skills that other people do not have. These skills can be traded for money which can be traded for goods, all of which are wealth.

There are natural assets such as oil, minerals, water, etc. They become potential wealth when someone, using human assets such as knowledge, can convert them to materials that can benefit humankind.

Unfortunately, people always seem to think that only money is wealth. Cash, as wealth, is variable in value. During inflationary times, cash is worth less and less. During a recession or a depression, cash may be worth less than having the know-how and the seeds to grow edible plants in your backyard. During a complete collapse, cash is nearly worthless.

Here is a semi-fictional interchange based on an actual conversation I had with a high school student many decades ago. Said student was bemoaning the idea that he earned nearly $100 a week pumping gas but never could take that amount home. Not only were taxes and social security extricated before he saw his check, but he had to buy gas to get to and from work. He also had to buy coveralls and hard work shoes in order to be able to work there.

"If you had been able to keep more, what would you have spent it on?" I asked.

"I'd take my girl out to an expensive restaurant and go down to Paragon Park on the weekend. You know, just have fun."

"That sounds quite typical for your age. You should have fun. However, you should also recognize that you are trading your wealth for experiences and not for other wealth."

"What do you mean?"

"If you invested 10 or 20 percent, you might have to go to a less fancy restaurant, but your money would accrue interest so that in a few years you would have enough monetary wealth to trade for other things that are less consumable. You know, like higher education."

"But that's consumable, isn't it?"

"If you chose the right institution and the right subjects, it would be an investment. In other words, the knowledge and skills you gain would be tradable for a job that pays even more. The money you earned would eventually be tradable for a house, and of course, other fun things, as well. In other words, you need to start thinking not only in terms of what you want to consume, but also the non-monetary wealth you want to build. You'll still have to buy gas and pay taxes, but you'll have a greater income and more to show for it."

We can count our money but it is much more difficult to count our wealth. That's one of the advantages of having a monetary system—so that a numeric value can be put on the kinds of wealth that are difficult to calculate. Numeric values of both tangible and non-tangible wealth are not sacrosanct nor are they identical from person to person, but without a numeric value with which to negotiate transactions, we'd be stuck with subjective values such as "I value this highly, semi-highly, moderately, kinda-sorta, and ah-not-so-much" and want to trade for something you value as "quite a lot, not a little, or ah-not quite".

Values are subjective, of course, but note that even those people that advocate for subjective realities seem to prefer the type of wealth that is the least sub-jective—money.

One advantage of living in a relatively free country is that anyone can choose to work for the type of wealth he/she prefers and not the type of wealth that one's neighbor prefers. One of the hallmarks of freedom is that a person is allowed to have his/her own values.

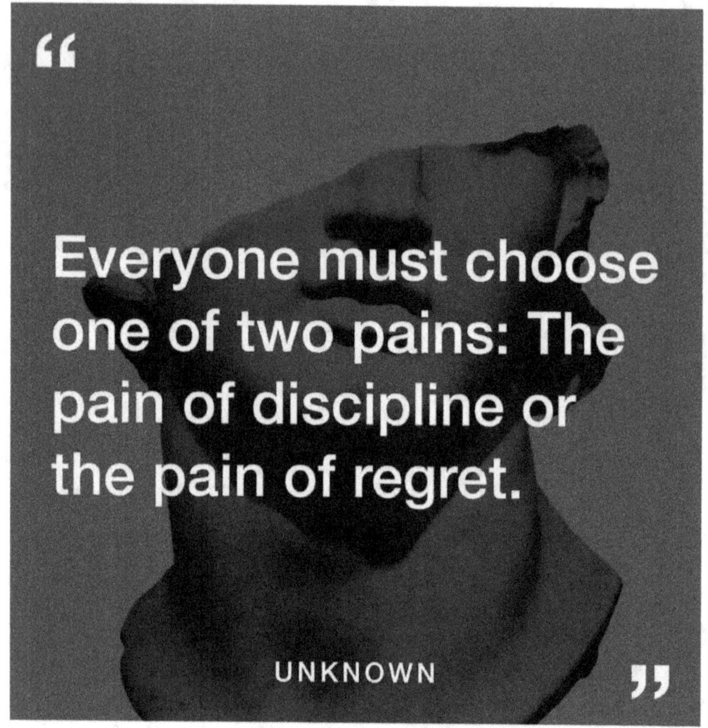
"
Everyone must choose one of two pains: The pain of discipline or the pain of regret.

UNKNOWN
"

# 9. Idiosyncratic Behavior ≠ Idiotic Behavior but Mentally Erratic Behavior ≠ Just a Passionate Commitment

If you were a straight laced schoolmarm from 19th century Boston, almost all idiosyncrasies would seem mentally ill to you. There would be, in your mind, one acceptable set of behaviors and every other action would either an ignorant error that must be immediately corrected (perhaps with a slap on the wrist) or it meant that you should be forcibly detained in a mental health facility, not only for your own wellbeing but also for the safety of society. If, however, you were a 19th century Boston schoolmarm who was marching for women's right to vote, you would not want your passionate commitment, although unusual in your culture, to be considered mentally erratic.

In fact, you may have wanted to rid the country of another "mentally erratic behavior" called intoxication, so you might have also wanted to advocate for temperance.

Consider the following scenario. A man goes to a bar after work, is depressed about his job, has no love interest, and no hobbies or other distractions. He finds himself drinking a little too much and sways his way out of the door and into the stability of his automobile. He is just aware enough to know that he should not drive, but also knows it will take hours to semi-detox. Is he behaving in a mentally erratic manner or is he simply acting idiosyncratically? Should he be punished by the state,  refused admission to the bar, refused liquor at the bar, or simply left alone to detox? Most of us would opt for his being left alone and perhaps being cut off by the bartender. Almost no one would opt for a legal punishment.

Now let's rework the details somewhat. The man drinks too much, sways out of the bar, bumping into both servers and customers, cuts across the parking lot, forcing vehicles to stop short in order not to hit him, and makes it to his car. Should he be punished by the state, refused admission to the bar, refused liquor at the bar, or simply left alone? Your answer may be the same as in the first scenario, but it is more likely that either someone from the bar will try to take him into the backroom to help him dry out or that some customer will call the police in order to make sure the man is not going to attempt to drive.

Another variation. The man drinks too much, gets rowdy and loud, and won't leave when asked to exit. He sloppily swears at the customer next to him but never gets violent. In essence, he is making a scene and his actions are unpredictable. Time to call in John Law? Probably. Why is there a law against being drunk and disorderly? Why is it that Orderly seems virtuous but Disorderly (in public) is not seen as just a Passionate Commitment to an Idiosyncratic Behavior? Could it be because everyone recognizes "normal" behavior and thus the lawmakers use "normal" as a norm around which to fashion laws on public misbehavior?

Now let's take one more scenario. Stanley Q. Clugmeister shows up to his office, where he works as a clerk, in a skirt and high heels. He is clearly breaching the norms for men's attire in his office, but in his job, he never has to interface with the public so he believe that his idiosyncratic behavior is simply an expression of his personal tastes. He likes to challenge gender norms and cross-dresses all the time at home, so why shouldn't a little skirt and heels be tolerated by his coworkers? Besides, last Friday his coworker Johnnie C. Laytelay wore a sports coat and turtleneck instead of a suit coat with shirt and tie even though the management had not as yet allowed for a casual Friday. Do his coworkers tolerate his fetish? I suspect that they do not. Nor does the management. At best, he will be advised to wear men's attire when showing up in a professional environment. At worst, he will be fired. Because he did not accept the pain of self-discipline, he will have to accept the pain of regret (as well as joblessness). Are they being intolerant of Stanley's passionate commitment to mixed gender attire? Or is Stanley being intentional inconsiderate of certain customs, even though they are unwritten?

At what point, when exercised in a business setting, will Stanley's unusual pastime be considered mentally erratic instead of merely idiosyncratic? Would he be disciplined simply because he broke the office rules or because he broke them in a way that challenges the norms and traditions of the wider society? Since every business has rules for its employees, if Stanley were disciplined because he flaunted its rules, everyone would understand. To disagree would encourage everyone to behave in his/her own way at his/her own hours, doing whatever he/she wanted. What if Stan were disciplined because his hobby is so far off the societal norm that most everyone would call it fetishistic? A loud minority in society would suggest that his fetish is simply being true to an "alternative lifestyle" in which he celebrates his "true self", and to oppose his behavior is to deny him freedom, i.e. to deny him his rights. That loud minority essentially wishes no rules for anyone so that any libertine behavior becomes so acceptable that it soon would become common.

**Oh, no, dear author. I must object! We just want Stanley to be accepted as he truly is.**

Then why isn't it good enough to be "as he truly is" at home? After all, no one in the office acts "as he/she truly is" in the office. They act they way they are supposed to act to get the job done. Somehow Stanley's version of "as he truly is" has to be brought into the office so as to alter the rules and conventions that make the office run smoothly, and yet no one else brings their pet Orangutan to work or yodels their communications because they have a Swiss heritage.

I am sure that psychologists can draw a narrower margin separating idiosyncratic from idiotic (in the "mentally ill" sense) than can average citizens; however, the average citizen's wider margin is not an affront to personal idiosyncrasies or even mentally erratic behavior. Rather, it is called "societal convention". Many of us really would like to change those conventions as we think them to be archaic or intolerant. Okay. Now the question is: How do we go about creating a change that is fair to everyone's sensibilities and will endure?

The first step, of course, is simply expressing a nonconformist opinion.

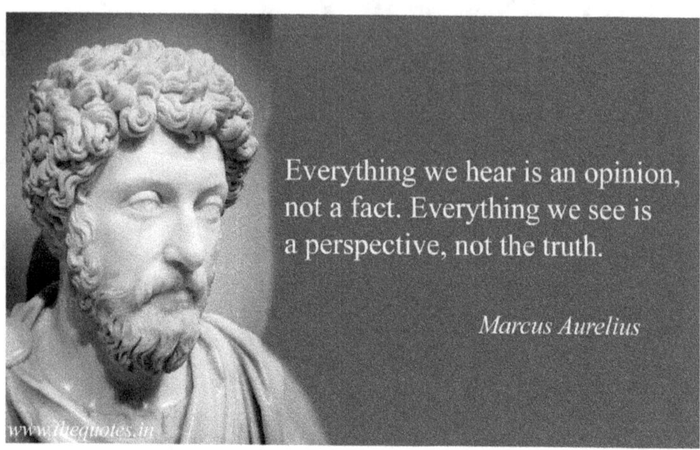
Everything we hear is an opinion,
not a fact. Everything we see is
a perspective, not the truth.

Marcus Aurelius

www.thequotes.in

# 10. Freely Expressed Opinions ≠ Valid Facts

With the advent of Facebook, Twitter, and other online social media, people have a greater opportunity than ever to express themselves—and to a much larger audience. Unfortunately, they cannot always choose that audience. Before social media, if you chose to express your political opinion, for example, you would do so only among like-minded friends or among friends who intended to have a political discussion. Quite unlike in social media, your best friend's third cousin would not be present and your buddies from the gym would not have been invited since it was your wife's or husband's boss who was throwing the party in which the discussion occurred. Thus, you freely expressed your opinion in a rather controlled group.

No one knew if his/her arguments had convinced anyone else, or even gave anyone else pause. The discussion was had, the opinions were expressed, and then you moved on to dessert, coffee, and playing Charades.

If, during the discussion, you had offered empirical data and established statistics as part of your argument, it is unlikely that you footnoted those sources. It is more likely that, informed or not, you simply offered your opinion freely so that others could add to it or counter it, and you could feel validated or adjust your point of view.

After the social gathering, if you were really interested in the topic, you might research the newly presented information at the library or review it with friends who knew more than you about the topic. The free expression of those other people's opinions either rankled you because they did not agree with you, or it gave you an impetus to validate the facts.

Today, most people on social media pick arguments with your best friend's third cousin or your partner's boss because they have no direct social relationship with you and have no need to retain your friendship. Rather, their need is to be correct. Thus, they treat their feely expressed opinion as if it were valid fact, backed by empirical data, and thus undeniable truth. So do you.

A moment's thought would confirm that any opinion, no matter where it is proffered, is not per force a fact validated by careful research and empirical evidence. And yet you and everyone else seem to want intellectual validation by vote of "LIKES" or "THUMBS UP", as if truth were subject to democratic ballot. Worse still, in my humble opinion (which must be factual since it is freely expressed as my own), is that the arguments used to win those social media votes are often not intellectual arguments at all, but clever ways of insulting the opposition, while trying to make moral points by making emotional assertions rather than offering empirical evidence or rational reasoning.

Ultimately, we use the disguise of intellectual argumentation in an attempt to appear morally superior. If we can't win enough votes to feel intellectually validated, we claim the other side is racist, fascist, uncaring, insensitive, and downright archaic in its thinking. Thus we act offended because if you can't win by intellectual superiority, you can always feign moral superiority because your tender sensibilities have been bruised.

PHILOSOPHICAL RHYTHMS

" Our worst enemies here are not
the ignorant and simple, however
cruel; our worst enemies are the
intelligent and corrupt."

~ Graham Greene

# 11. Being Offended ≠ Moral Superiority

People who easily get their feelings hurt have evidently grown up in a softly cushioned chamber, which to me is akin to a rubber room. It is not just that they are sensitive; it is that they think their sensitivity means that *you must have* offended them, thus you are an offensive person, and thus by comparison, they are morally superior. Is this behavior crazy or just a freely expressed opinion masquerading as a valid fact? Since no one can discern the objective truth about subjective feelings, how can you know if you really offended them? And if you did, might it have been accidentally? And no matter how you might have offended them, does that make you a bad person? Or are they being just a little disingenuous, hypersensitive, hyper-vigilant, and/or verging on the idiotic?

Perhaps their tendency to look for ways to be offended is simply idiosyncratic behavior which, as we have discussed, is not idiotic behavior. Maybe it is just a passionate commitment to a way of life. That way of life, however, may be less than optimal in terms of getting along with others or actually achieving a level of morality. It artificially shields the offended from any criticism, since the offended party chooses to see criticism as harassment.

In my book *Petulant*, I discuss various ways in which many people who make political arguments have borrowed from pre-feminist argumentation, i.e. trying to win by emotionally beating down the opponent rather than by proving him wrong. The simple trick to this style of petulant argumentation is simply to assume that the opponent never can be right (since he is not you) and will always do something objectionable, even if his arguments seem valid. And that validity is to be denied or avoided at all costs.

Recently, I streamed an Australian TV show called *Wolf Like Me*. Whether or not you like this kind of werewolf-in-contemporary-sheep's-clothing drama, I suggest watching the opening scene of episode one, the luncheon date in which an angry girlfriend is trying to break up with her previously widowed boyfriend who is occupied with his emotionally challenged daughter. Within a few minutes, she shows that petulant argumentation is based on always being the victim and pretending to stand up for yourself in the face of overwhelming odds *(the male is much bigger than she and, after all, possesses the toxic hormone testosterone)*. Thus, the offended party becomes both morally superior and heroic—but only to herself (and to any of her close friends whom she can convince of her male opponent's dastardliness). To most objective observers, she is unnecessarily self-centered, annoying, irreconcilable, unapproachable, and well...petulant.

Acting as if you were offended by an unrecorded and unvocalized list of actions ends up itself being offensive. By this standard then, your acting offended, i.e. using being offended as a ploy, is itself offensive to your alleged offender and thus makes him, not you, morally superior.

In today's world, people would rather find ways to be offended than work at actually increasing their moral stature. It is difficult to maintain ethical behavior at all times and in every circumstance, but it is easy to get upset at someone else's words, tone of voice, bearing, posture, attitude, or circumstance. It's an attempt at moral superiority without even trying to be moral!

Because being insulted can happen to anyone and because, in a relatively free society, anyone can find anyone else's behavior offensive, in the early and middle part of the twentieth century, people used religion and strong social pressure to get the offensive to conform. In the late sixties that movement toward compelling conformity changed to a call for tolerance. Toleration and social change went hand-in-hand. In contemporary times (c. 2023), people have employed the social pressure to be tolerant as a method to get away with whatever they wish while at the same time calling those who disagree "intolerant".

In an effort to prove moral superiority, social causes are not only advocated, not only adopted and contributed to, but also opponents of the cause are labeled as troglodytes or immoral actors. Facts don't matter when the cause gives its supporters a reason to feel superior. No discussion about opposing empirical data can be tolerated. Their cause's imagined and desired truth must be equal to a universally accepted objective truth. If their "truth" is not at least widely accepted, they will quietly find another cause to be righteous about. Instead of doing the hard research to feel confident that they are right, they prefer to start by knowing they are right and select the data that support what they "know" to be true. This "my truth first, supporting facts later" method is not just to save the downtrodden or rejuvenate the planet; it is to give them an enemy to oppose so that they can feel righteous. [See *Your Ethics are Immoral* for more on this.] Even when the offense is felt or the cause has some validity, they practice using

intellectual slight-of-hand to corrupt the idea of objec-
tivity in order to feel morally, and sometime intellectually, superior.

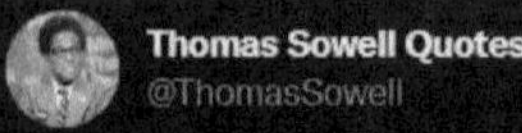

Thomas Sowell Quotes
@ThomasSowell
Everybody is an environmentalist in the sense of not wanting to breathe polluted air or drink polluted water. But in practice the term has come to refer to a pagan nature worship cult that readily sacrifices other human beings on the altar to their dogmas.
1:00 PM · Aug 21, 2022 · Twitter for iPhone

# 12. Climate Change ≠ Climate Crisis

For decades, I have been waiting for the climate crisis to rear its ugly head in more than a solo weather event that neither repeats itself nor falls into a pattern. Since I am not a climatologist nor do I play one on TV, I am not about to compare the statistics of the legitimately scared fear-mongers to those who think there is a problem but we'll have to rush to fix it, to those who think there is a problem but that is not a crisis, or to those who think it is a scam and the scam is the real crisis. However, I hope to use this long-lived "cause" as an example of Being Offended ≠ Moral Superiority in a way that leads me to the next chapter about journalism.

First, let me acknowledge that in some areas at some time, the weather creates a catastrophic problem. No one can deny that hurricanes, tornadoes, and volcano eruptions are real, and when they occur, they bring enormous devastation. Volcano eruptions happen rarely but active volcanoes throughout the world are monitored to determined if an eruption is likely to occur. Hurricanes and tornadoes happen with predictable frequency in predictable areas. If you live on the gulf coast of Louisiana or Florida, you are not surprised if a hurricane comes your way. If you live in northern Texas, Oklahoma, Kansas, or Missouri, you are not surprised if tornado sirens go off. There are pre-built shelters in which to secure yourself. They were pre-built because when settling in Tornado Alley, people consciously balanced the low costs and open plains to the risk of destructive storms. No one had to convince you there was a climate threat in your area. You already knew that, but settled or remained there despite the risk. If the risk became worse, you'd more willingly consider moving.

| YEAR | TORNADOES | FATALITIES |
| --- | --- | --- |
| 2014 | 41 | 0 |
| 2015 | 17 | 0 |
| 2016 | 39 | 0 |
| 2017 | 51 | 0 |
| 2018 | 108 | 1 |
| 2019 | 85 | 0 |
| 2020 | 38 | 0 |
| 2021 | 28 | 1 |
| 2022 | 19 | – |

Data source: https://www.ncei.noaa.gov/access/monitoring/tornadoes/
[chart modified from original only in order of years]

Note that there was a large increase of tornadoes in 2018, but that the total number of tornadoes has diminished from 2014 to 2022. This is not a large enough selection to determine a pattern, however. When you trace the statistics back to 1969, the total number of tornadoes increases until 1985 and then decreases until 1990 when it surges upward again and then decreases again in 2012. It goes up again in 2015 and down again in 2018. In other words, there is no discernible steady increase.

How about hurricanes?

See the following chart:

| Decade | Saffir-Simpson Category 1 | | | | | All 1,2,3,4,5 | Major 3,4,5 |
|---|---|---|---|---|---|---|---|
| | 1 | 2 | 3 | 4 | 5 | | |
| 1851-1860 | 8 | 5 | 5 | 1 | 0 | 19 | 6 |
| 1861-1870 | 8 | 6 | 1 | 0 | 0 | 15 | 1 |
| 1871-1880 | 7 | 6 | 7 | 0 | 0 | 20 | 7 |
| 1881-1890 | 8 | 9 | 4 | 1 | 0 | 22 | 5 |
| 1891-1900 | 8 | 5 | 5 | 3 | 0 | 21 | 8 |
| 1901-1910 | 10 | 4 | 4 | 0 | 0 | 18 | 4 |
| 1911-1920 | 10 | 4 | 4 | 3 | 0 | 21 | 7 |
| 1921-1930 | 5 | 3 | 3 | 2 | 0 | 13 | 5 |
| 1931-1940 | 4 | 7 | 6 | 1 | 1 | 19 | 8 |
| 1941-1950 | 8 | 6 | 9 | 1 | 0 | 24 | 10 |
| 1951-1960 | 8 | 1 | 5 | 3 | 0 | 17 | 8 |
| 1961-1970 | 3 | 5 | 4 | 1 | 1 | 14 | 6 |
| 1971-1980 | 6 | 2 | 4 | 0 | 0 | 12 | 4 |
| 1981-1990 | 9 | 1 | 4 | 1 | 0 | 15 | 5 |
| 1991-2000 | 3 | 6 | 4 | 0 | 1 | 14 | 5 |
| 2001-2004 | 4 | 2 | 2 | 1 | 0 | 9 | 3 |
| **1851-2004** | 109 | 72 | 71 | 18 | 3 | 273 | 92 |
| **Average Per Decade** | 7.1 | 4.7 | 4.6 | 1.2 | 0.2 | 17.7 | 6.0 |

1 Only the highest Saffir-Simpson Category to affect the U.S. has been used. This is taken from NOAA Technical Memorandum NWS TPC-4:

THE DEADLIEST, COSTLIEST, AND MOST INTENSE UNITED STATES HURRICANES FROM 1851 TO 2004
by Eric S. Blake, Jerry D. Jarrell(retired) and Edward N. Rappaport
NOAA/NWS/ Tropical Prediction Center; Miami, Florida

Can you detect any pattern or regular increase over 154 years?

What about record-breaking heat or cold? There seems to a pattern here. *Climate.gov* reports:

Earth's temperature has risen by 0.14° Fahrenheit (0.08° Celsius) per decade since 1880, but the rate of warming since 1981 is more than twice that: 0.32° F (0.18° C) per decade.

 • 2021 was the sixth-warmest year on record based on NOAA's temperature data.

 • Averaged across land and ocean, the 2021 surface temperature was 1.51 °F (0.84 °Celsius) warmer than the twentieth-century average of 57.0 °F (13.9 °C) and 1.87 °F (1.04 °C) warmer than the pre-industrial period (1880-1900).

 • The nine years from 2013 through 2021 rank among the 10 warmest years on record.

So the concept of Climate Change, at its core, seems to be about Global Warming (it's original title). Most research links the increase in temperature to increased carbon emissions. Carbon emissions, in turn, are allegedly due to human activities. And in fact, there is a parallel between the growth of those emissions and various human activities like driving. But are humans the primary or even the dominant cause of carbon emissions?

The very plants which absorb CO2 may also be the cause of a large percentage of that very CO2. Decaying plants produce a significant amount of carbon.

A new study involving ANU and international collaborators has found plants release more carbon dioxide into the atmosphere through respiration than expected.

Plants use photosynthesis to capture carbon dioxide and then release half of it into the atmosphere through respiration. Plants also release oxygen into the atmosphere through photosynthesis.

Professor Owen Atkin from ANU said the study revealed that the release of carbon dioxide by plant respiration around the world is up to 30 per cent higher than previously predicted.

He said the carbon dioxide released by plants every year was now estimated to be about 10 to 11 times the emissions from human activities, rather than the previous estimate of five to eight times.

SOURCE: https://www.anu.edu.au/news/

Carbon dioxide via plant respiration was 30% more than predicted. But "more" and "less" are relative terms. If CO2 is the main culprit, who or what is to blame for excess CO2? Should we junk our gasoline powered automobiles and make a run for the nearest EV (Electric Vehicle) Dealership, despite the fact that the creation of EVs cause more pollution per car than fossil fuels, and despite the fact that their batteries cannot be easily recycled?

Here's a graph from the EPA (Environmental Protection Agency):

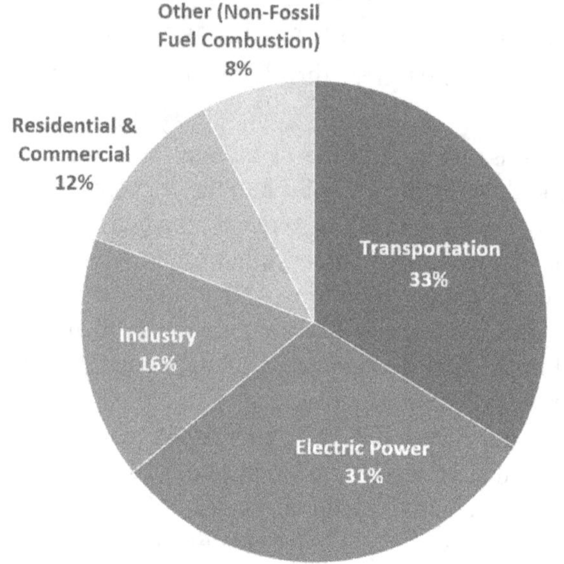


SOURCE: https://www.epa.gov/ghgemissions/overview-greenhouse-gases

If this piechart is accurate, use of electricity (often powered by fossil fuels) in transportation would not reduce CO2 emissions over transportation powered by fossil fuels. What if we had different sources of power for our homes and businesses? Windmills require large swaths of land to be cleared in order to set them up, and they do not work without wind or in freezing temperatures. Solar panels are not biodegradable and function when there only is direct sunlight.

All of this assumes that (1) warming is the prime issue, (2) that CO2 is the prime source of the warming, and (3) that human action is the prime source of that CO2. But by many accounts, the climate "crisis" is a function of many factors, not just weather patterns, and not simply human transportation or power use.

John Cristy, Professor of Atmospheric Science and Director of the Earth System Science Center at the University of Alabama, writes:

> And so, other than the fact that sea level is rising a bit, the extreme events are just not there to start to really cause problems. Now we are in a problem of having greater damages occur because of extreme events, and that's mainly because we've just built so much more stuff and placed it in harm's way. Our coastlines are crowded with condominiums and entertainment parks and retirement villages and so on. There's so many more of them that when a hurricane does come, well, it's going to wipe out a lot more. And so, sure, the absolute value of those damages has gone up, but the number of hurricanes, their strength and so on, the background climate has not caused that problem. It's just that we like to build things in places that are dangerous.

SOURCE: https://www.biznews.com/energy/2022/12/12/climate-crisis

Cristy points to the bottom line that a lot of Climate Crisis advocates ignore. Hotter or colder, *how does the changing weather effect human beings?*

Judith Curry, chair of the School of Earth and Atmospheric Sciences at the Georgia Institute of Technology, writes:

But if you look at the data there, it says [so]. Most people just look at the data from 1950 or 1970. The 1970s and 1980s was a relatively benign period of weather. And so, if you just do the trend since 1970, "Oh, the weather is worse now". Well, yes, but it's not worse than the 1930s or 40s or even the 50s. And people are much more prosperous. Globally, poverty is way down. Life expectancy is up. We're doing very well as we reduce poverty and human development advances. A lot of that has been fueled by petroleum and coal. Are there better fuels out there? Well, hopefully in the future there will be advanced nuclear and stuff like that, very promising advanced geothermal. But right now, this minute, having our entire energy infrastructure relying on wind turbines and solar energy is going to cause a lot of harm to a lot of people, not just to the overall economy. You can't run an industrial economy on wind and solar, at least not in the way it's currently envisioned. It requires a huge land footprint.

People haven't thought this out and there's no emergency. Economically, we're all expected to be four times better off worldwide by the end of the 21st century. And a little bit of that might be shaved off because of damages from global warming. But we're all going to be better off moving forward through the 21st century unless we do really stupid stuff like destroy our energy infrastructure before we have something better to replace it with. That's the biggest danger. The biggest climate risk right now is a so-called transition risk; the risk of rapidly getting rid of fossil fuels. I'm no fan of pollution and crazy price spikes and whatever. I'd love to see inexpensive, cleaner, reliable, secure energy, better than what we have now. But going to 100% renewables is not a better solution.

SOURCE: https://www.biznews.com/global-citizen/2022/10/05/climate-change-2

Have I mentioned above that Expertise ≠ Accuracy? But I am no expert, so I could be wrong, couldn't I? Of course! However, wouldn't it make sense to estimate the importance of a claimed crisis by looking at the record of the boy who cried, "Wolf!"?

1960's - Oil gone in 10 years

1970's - another ice age in 10 years

1980's - acid rain will destroy all crops in 10 years

1990's - The ozone layer will be destroyed in 10 years

2000's - The icecaps will be gone in 10 years

None happened, but all resulted in more taxes.

So, if the record of disaster predictions is so inaccurate, why do we continue to accept disaster forecasts? I suspect that it is because those who report on these ideas can sell more print space and airtime when the news is emotionally jarring. The headline can never be "No Climate Crisis Exists Right Now and We'll Be Okay in the Future". Even if it sold newspapers, or made people watch a podcast, it would do so just once. It could not be milked for an indefinite period of time, nor would it provide an enemy to rail against.

Perhaps the idea of "all news is bad news" has existed for far longer than we have had a 24/7 news cycle, but what did not exist in the past was the idea that if news were really objective, we'd not make any money.

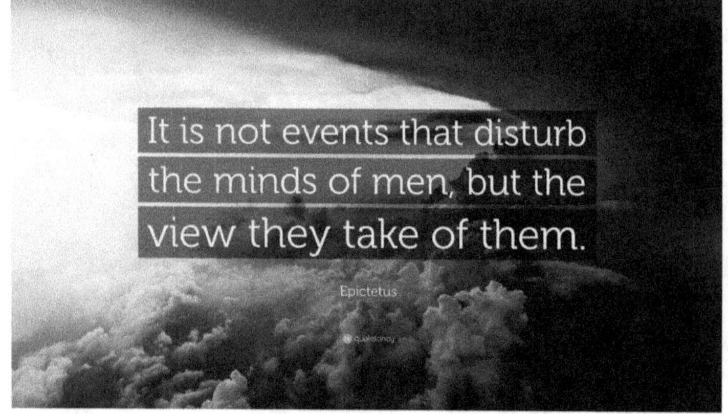
It is not events that disturb
the minds of men, but the
view they take of them.
Epictetus

# 13. Journalism ≠ Reportage

With newspapers and magazines still alive, with legacy and cable news stations as well as Internet news sites going strong, there are more journalists than ever before, and the reportage is abundant. But is the journalism of the average reporter truly reportage? Are journalists objectively reporting what happens or editing themselves and pre-selecting their stories in order to advance either a preferred agenda or an exciting and controversial topic that will catch an audience? Are they more concerned with discerning what truly is news or presenting a topic in a way that is fast, easy, and fills the news slot of the day?

In junior high school, we studied newspapers, notably the *New York Times, The Boston Globe,* which were then separate companies, and *The Boston Herald.* We studied the informational structure of the stories, the headlines and sub-headlines. Then the teacher briefly mentioned that a story would not be published unless it's writer had three separate, unrelated sources to verify it. A decade or so into the new millennium, during a TV news discussion program, a commentator was bemoaning that idea that, in "the old days", a reporter would need to have at least two independent sources for his/her story. Either I had been misinformed as a youth or the standards for valid news stories had dropped by 33%.

In those old days, reporters were eager to get on the scene in order to "scoop" their competition. Their competition was on the scene as well, sometimes earlier than they, sometimes later. However, almost always a story in one newspaper would read similarly to a story in another. The news was the news.

Hard-nosed reporters gradually gave way to college graduates with journalism degrees that weren't as tough or eager to work, but were quite clever in how they wrote a story. Instead of having Who, What, Where, Why, and How, we had a little paragraph to set a mood and then the beginning of a tale that might be told in a novel. Eventually, the story would get to the news, but not before showing off the creative writing skills of the "reporter". News became less newsy and more creative.

Newspapers were gradually giving way to TV News, the stations of which did not send out reporters from a central city office, but had correspondents stationed all around the country, and later in major cities across the globe, in case relevant or important news broke out anywhere near them. Because the TV news appeared four times a day, morning, noon, suppertime, and late evening, one main story might be repeated four times so that early or late viewers got a chance to see it. Editorials, if they occurred, happened only during the last few minutes of the newscast. There was no way to determine whether the anchor was on the Left or the Right until then. Sometimes, there were even 2-person give-and-take sessions during the editorial segment so that viewers could understand opposing points-of-view.

Then came the advent of cable news and the 24/7 new cycle. How many times can you report the same items every day? Instead of straight reporting, we got commentary. Perhaps viewers would be more interested in one person's unique perspective on these items, or perhaps they would like panel discussions that they used to see only on Sunday news shows. But still, wouldn't there have to be a lot of repetition? How would the cable news stations fill the time and still entertain enough so that viewers would return and the ratings would go up?

First job: we have to find more news. How can

we possibly do that? We already have correspondents on Capitol Hill, at The White House, and in every state capitol. Well, how do magazines get people to buy another issue month after month or week after week? The most popular weekly magazines at the supermarket are Hollywood gossip rags. They provide a potential model for a successful 24/7 cable network! But we can't talk too much about Hollywood. It's got to be more about politics, politicians, or crap that common citizens do that might interest other people or get them angry. Or we could emphasize stories that might interest governments, even if they are not supposed to be interested in what free people do. Okay, so how do we get this kind of information?

Social media.

Social media will inform us about what the average person is thinking, how he/she feels about it, and also what common disagreements we can emphasize to ramp up the excitement of a "news" story. Social media allows us to keep our fingers on the pulse of the citizen while not even leaving the office. No need to have three or even two story confirmations; there will be dozens in the commentary section of each post. Even better, somebody will come up with a clever and sarcastic phrase we can use for a headline or in a non-editorial (but covertly editorial) paragraph. You know, something like "Sources say that former representative Clipton

Clowers—now fortressing himself on Wolverton Mountain—not only has a lovely young daughter, but also that he is mighty handy with a gun and a knife. What do these sources tell us? They say don't go to Wolverton Mountain. Especially if you are looking for a wife."

But is that really news? It is now. Think of the danger Mr. Clowers potentially provides with previous government standing, his male patriarchy, and his lack of gun control. News exists where you find it or where you make it.

Such news fills the 24-hour cycle and satisfies both our viewers and our advertisers. Although it does not report on facts, it does create new and ever more exciting conflicts. And that's what sells.

By creating the news or emphasizing one aspect over another (in other words, by refusing to be objective), journalists are willing to foment conflict in society in order to earn a paycheck. News organizations are eager to employ "journalists" who are good at fomenting conflict in order to get viewers. Viewers attract advertisers. But at what cost? A popularity that is earned is laudable in most cases, but a popularity that is manipulated in order to reap the monetary benefits that popularity brings is disingenuous at best, and at worse, sacrifices social unity for personal (albeit undeserved) profit.

In the USA, we have a divided country not simply because 50% of the country is on the Left and 50% on the Right. We have a divided country because we cannot agree on the truth. We cannot agree on the truth because those agencies on which we depend to inform us are not objective, fair, or evenhanded. As a result, social unity continues to escape us, even though our principles and values are often more aligned than we think (see my book *10 Common Values*).

As a result, some citizens and many activists think that not only can they compel unity, but also that they must compel unity. To do so, they have to dominate. To dominate, they have to make one side look misanthropic, or at least misinformed.

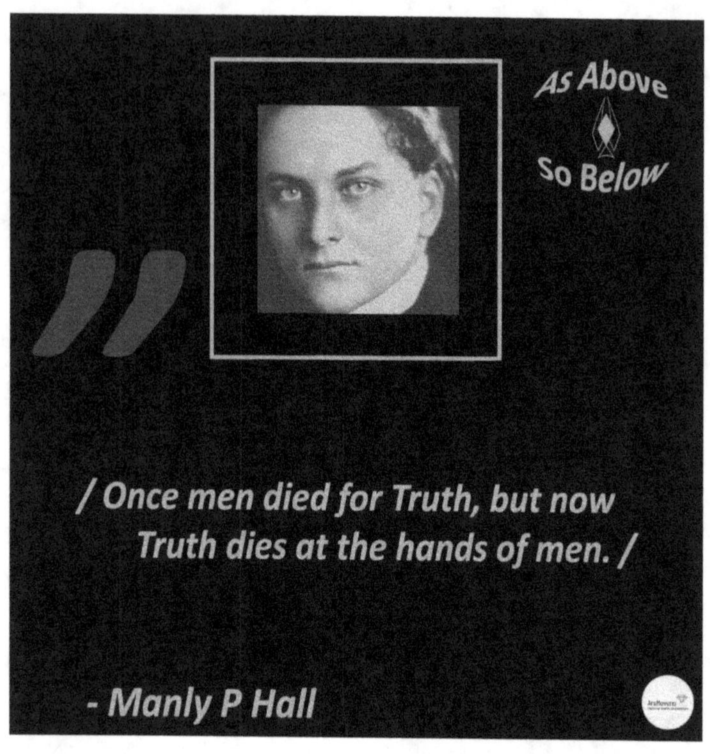
As Above
So Below
/ Once men died for Truth, but now
Truth dies at the hands of men. /
- Manly P Hall

# 14. Opposing Opinions ≠ Misinformation

*Mis*information is untrue data understood to be true, perhaps accidentally. *Dis*information is untrue data intentionally portrayed as true to deceive people.

Over the last year or so (2020-22), we have repeatedly heard the charge that certain published papers, broadcasts, Internet blogs, and social media posts promulgate "misinformation". The government, always with the best interests of their citizens at heart, no doubt, allegedly does not want people to believe falsehoods, either because those people would vote for the wrong candidate, or because they would not believe the experts that the government puts forth to keep the people well-informed. In other words, the government wants you not to think for yourself.

Whether or not you liked President Trump, there is no doubt that his opponents spread false information about him. He was not an agent of Russia, a racist, or a Nazi, for example.

When CoVid-19 came along, we were told it came from a Chinese wet market. The idea that it may have escaped from a virology laboratory was supposed to be misinformation. To say so, or even ask about it, was racist. But it did "escape" from The Wuhan Institute of Virology, and no, we are not racists.

We were told that wearing masks and keeping six feet apart from each other would help prevent the dissemination of the virus. Those who disagreed were considered dangerous and spreaders of misinformation. Then we found out that, in fact, there was absolutely no research to back up the functionality of social distancing or the effectiveness of normal masks that people commonly wear. High school science would tell us that viruses are much, much smaller than bacterias and thus could easily slip through cloth masks. But if we said that, we were "science-deniers".

We were told that lockdowns were necessary to prevent the spread of the virus, even though they would destroy businesses and set children's social and educational development back at least a year. But the science-deniers who claimed we were on the wrong track were misinforming everyone else. Sweden did not lockdown and it fared better than countries that did. China locked down with severely draconian measures and, at the end of 2022, had the greatest number of new CoVid cases.

We were told that the Project Warp Speed vaccines were going to be the solution to the pandemic. Vaccine doubters were spreading misinformation. But now we find that these vaccines neither prevented the spread nor the contracting of CoVid.

We were told that CoVid was a pandemic of the unvaccinated. Then we found that more people died from CoVid having taken the vaccines than those who did not take the vaccines.

Details about possible illegal governmental pay-offs on Hunter Biden's laptop were suppressed by the FBI, both through news networks not covering the story at the FBI's request and through social media outlets claiming any posts discussing the possibility of corruption was Russian disinformation. Now that the 2020 election is over, we find that gradually some elements of the laptop story are coming out. There was no Russian disinformation; however, the American voters were misinformed through the *absence* of information.

Certainly misinformation and disinformation exist. However, in today's world, the term "misinformation" is used to silence opposing points-of-view without so much as a counterargument. My rules of thumb are these: (1) if someone calls it misinformation, I want to hear that misinformation myself. I want to decide myself whether a piece of data deserves further investigation and I want to choose for myself the sources at which I research that information; (2) if someone calls me a choice epithet simply because I want to know the information he/she considers false, it is likely that the information isn't as false as he/she would like me to believe.

If news agencies cannot be trusted to report fully, to be objective, or to present both sides of a story and if government officials care more about being obeyed than citizens being able to decide things for themselves, how then is unity to proceed? And should some politician or aficionado of some philosophy jump up and down volunteering to unify us, will it really be the kind of unity we were hoping for?

> "The urge to save humanity is almost always a false front for the urge to rule it."
>
> – H.L Mencken

# 15. The Unity You Imagine ≠ The Unity You Will Get

Concomitant with the previous chapter, consider why "journalists" refuse to give people objective, unaltered facts. You may say it is because they have a political agenda of their own. Certainly, that has become true, but even if they hadn't, there are still other, perhaps more fundamental reasons. One of them is that, in free societies, those who satisfy the masses with what the masses want to hear or see are those who are popular.

People who denigrate capitalism often hold among their principles the idea that self-interested capitalists get rich feeding the people what they want even though what they want may not be good for them. Fair enough, although you never hear anti-capitalists talk about a central economy feeding people what they don't want even though it is not necessarily good for them. Critics of capitalism tend to ignore the self-interest aspect of a news organization feeding people what they want even if it is not good for them.

What if news organizations agreed to be unified in feeding the people what they allegedly want? Is that better? It seems that our journalists, as well as our leaders, have forgotten that neither money-making nor obedient unity to a narrative actually contributes to either a real sense of cultural unity or the collective well-being.

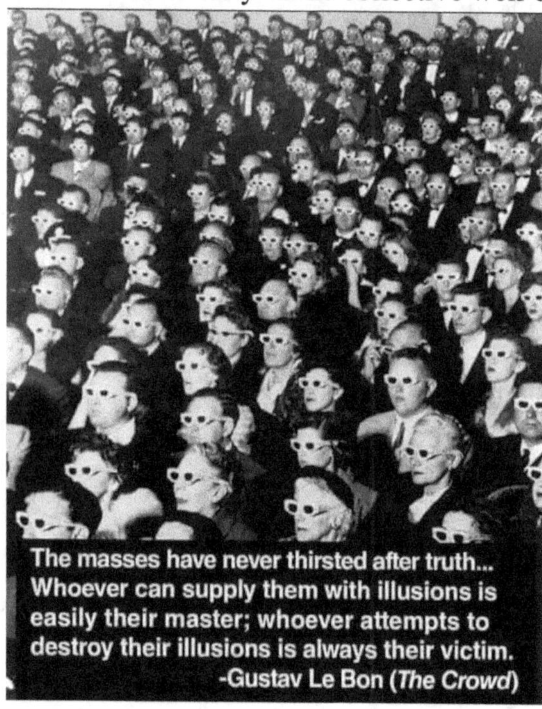

Idealists (which includes many social activists) are never satisfied with the current reality. They assume that their soon-to-be-created ideal reality will bring social perfection and personal satisfaction. But Idealism ≠ Realism. I mean this in two ways: (1) the real here-and-now is not perfect so clearly the current state of existence does not equal an ideal state of existence, and (2) idealists are seldom satisfied with even the new reality they may create since no reality can be perfect. There is no unbiased standard that will satisfy everyone equally.

Remember the first chapter on Equity ≠ Equality? Does anyone actually believe that any action by activists, by the state, or even collective voluntarism can result in a world where everyone would be the same? If magically that world could exist, would it be ideal?

Consider what actual, real-life unity might look like. To the extent that it has existed, it is pluralistic rather than universal and people accept that their unity is imperfect but as holistic as it realistically can be.

I suspect that the unity that people think they want is not a unity that can be achieved. I also believe that to the extent that some sort of unity can be achieved, it is not the unity with which idealists would be satisfied.

Everyone knows there is no such thing as perfection, but not everyone is content with simple improvement, even if that improvement were continuous and were to embrace a wider number of people as time went on.

Throughout history leaders have unified their peoples in one way or another. When the unity is voluntary and around a noble or ethical purpose, it functioned, never perfectly, but substantively enough to recognize a more desirable togetherness rather than the previous, less desirable contention.

Take for example Italy and its hero-unifier Giuseppe Garibaldi (1807-82). Italy in the 1800s was divided into approximately 20 city-states. Napoleon Bonaparte had ruled Italy as a "kingdom" since 1805.

In 1848, Garibaldi returned to Italy from South America.

> While in Brazil, Garibaldi became active in [Brazilian] politics, joining the cause of the Riogran-denese republic in the Ragamuffin War. The Raga-muffin war was a secession effort by the Brazilian state of Rio Grande de Sul. While the Ragamuffin war would last until 1845, Garibaldi abandoned the cause and in 1841...moved to Uruguay. Garibaldi got involved in the Uruguayan Civil War, supporting the rebelling Colorados. Garibaldi was a principal figure in the siege of Montevideo, helping the embattled city survive. In 1848, political agitation arose in Italy and Garibaldi felt it was time to return home....

> Sicily was in the midst of a revolt, which pre-sented the vacuum necessary for Garibaldi's plan. Garibaldi landed in Sicily with a thousand men ready to conquer the island and unite the country.

Garibaldi achieved several key victories and soon controlled the Island of Sicily. Garibaldi established a dictatorship there to temporarily rule and his forces soon cross[ed] into mainland Italy. When Garibaldi landed in Southern Italy, he was welcomed as a liberator and not as an enemy. When Garibaldi did meet opposition, his ragtag army dealt with them quickly and continued their march to Naples. At this point, Garibaldi overthrew the Kingdom of the Two Sicilies and was ready to capture the capital of Napoli. Most of Southern Italy was ready to join a united Italy along with the Kingdom of Piedmont-Sardinia. On the proverbial to-do list was to expel the Austrians in the North, take control of the papal states, and make Rome the capital of Italy. Garibaldi essentially captured all of Southern Italy and handed it over to Victor Emmanuel II, the man who would be the first King of Italy. Garibaldi's work was done. He played a principal role in the unification of Italy and without him would likely not have happened.

SOURCE: https://www.thehistorycorner.org/articles-by-the-team/the-father-of-modern-italy-giuseppe-garibaldi-and-the-italian-unification

Garibaldi's willingness to step away from his own dictatorship was unique among military unifiers. He created a generally positive unity because his goal was to overcome the rule of an invader.

Fast forward 70 or so years to Benito Mussolini (1883-1945). In the early 1920s, the Fascists seized power, dismantled democratic institutions, and Mussolini became Italy's dictator (officially, he was Prime Minister from 1922-1943). The idea of "Fascism" was to bind the cords of Italian society together so that they would be stronger, like threads of a rope combine to create a thick hawser. Today, Fascism is held to be as far to the Right as militant Socialism is to the Left; however, Mussolini not only fully embraced Socialism but also said that he would be a Socialist until his dying day. He coined the word "Totalitarianism", not to suggest dictatorship, but to imply an idealistic "equality for everyone", albeit under state guidelines. In practice, he was an authoritarian pragmatist, not simply doing what he thought was called for to benefit his country, but also believing that whatever he felt was called for was thereby morally correct.

His "reunification" of Italy and his powerful demeanor was lauded by people as seemingly unlike him as Winston Churchill (although Churchill may have done so because he thought Fascism less dangerous than Communism). During the depression, Franklin Delano Roosevelt thought that Mussolini was an excellent example of governance not by principle but by practicality. The New York Times and various academics were vocal in their praise of Mussolini. Not as brutal as some dictators, but more brutal than others, he was known for "getting things done". His attempt at strong-handed unification left the world with Fascism and an alliance with Adolph Hitler. What his venerators thought Mussolini would provide was not the only thing he provided, and not what they had expected. His unity may have existed, but it was strong-arm unity gained at great cost to the people of Italy and Europe.

Another example of unity with unforeseen consequences is the founder of Islam. Under Mohammed (570-632), Islamic armies tried to unify the Middle East for Allah. The result of that religious-military action is that today several countries' governments interpret the Koran as an ideology that is anti-democratic, anti-feminine, and anti-Western. There do exist dominantly Muslim counties that do not want to conquer non-Muslim countries, but those countries that are aggressive are the descendants of Mohammed's attempting to bring all people under his interpretation of what Allah really wanted. His unity worked to some extent, but also brought Jihad to the rest of the world.

Disappointment in the results of unifying a group of people does not have to be on such a grand scale. Consider office "team building". A business has set goals and its leaders want all employees to gear their efforts toward those goals. Makes sense. What if you found that you, as an employee, were working toward certain unstated goals. Or, what if you found that you were expected to employ dishonest means to reach agreed upon goals? Your team's unity might be solid, but its result would have been unexpectedly negative. Was Enron's corporate team unified in 2001 just before the huge financial scandal that resulted in its shares dropping from \$90 to \$1?

Whenever you are voluntarily a part of a group, you may find that the group eventually does not stand for what its mission statement alleges. What if you were part of a group such as a nationality, a religion, or a country, for which you did not volunteer. I suspect that you would prefer unity within that group, but not at the price of accepting beliefs or actions you did not wish to be part of. If you embraced your Venezuelan heritage as a youth, for example, you may have rethought your national pride when the country's political position severely changed. (See *The Collective Problem* for more on the individual and the group.)

Does this mean that those who advocate for cultural unity will always end up producing something worse? Of course not. But it does mean that you have to be careful what you wish for. And how you get there.

What kind of unity would be produced by those that, in this author's opinion, misuse the various words and phrases discussed in this book? If you fool yourself into believing that $A = B$ when a little careful thinking would prove to you that $A \neq B$, you are choosing to live a lie.

As regards the idea of unifying the country under a new way of thinking that is expressed by some of the words and phrases we have discussed, a quick review is in order.

**Equity ≠ Equality**
**Equality ≠ Identity:**

If equity (equality of results) existed, there would be no diversity. Unity would mean absolute identity, i.e. everyone would be the same, act the same, and think the same. Perfect robotic unity.

**Self-identity ≠ Actual Identity:**

If you could think yourself into being what you'd like to be, no one would think to challenge who you are. It would be obvious. However, now since agreement on who or what you are is not obvious, unity becomes difficult.

**Disparities ≠ Discrimination:**

If there were no natural disparities, there would be no diversity (see Equity ≠ Equality, above). Some disparities are undesirable, others are sought out. If I hit a record number of home runs in a season, there is a disparity between me and everyone else in the world. But it is not because of discrimination. To assume it is means constant class struggle. Struggle does not add to unity.

**Intelligence ≠ Rationality**
**Expertise ≠ Accuracy:**

Intelligence and expertise can simply be accumulated knowledge. However, you can compile inaccurate knowledge or you can amass accurate knowledge but not know how to use it. If you depend on someone's credentials without doing your own evaluation, you're asking to be led astray. Unity can exist among the followers of a trusted leader but distrust, due to a leader's poor accuracy record, is unlikely to promote unity.

**Riots ≠ Demonstrations**

**Mob Rule ≠ Democracy:**

If you need to riot in order to demonstrate for a cause, soon there will be no one who would support your cause. If a mob could determine what an organized society voted for, there would be no use for voting at all. In fact, because Might would make Right, no one could determine whether or not the mob really represented a majority. Unity would be elusive because there would always be a master group (often the minority) and a servant group (often the majority).

**A Democracy ≠ A Republic:**

If the majority ruled, but the minority had no rights, gradually members of the society would rebel, using mob rule to regain their rights. If the majority could keep the minority in check and continue to disallow them their rights, the government would be neither a democracy nor a republic, but an oligarchy or a family-run farm.

**License ≠ Liberty**

**Freedom to be Unconventional ≠ A Claim to Normality:**

If we were all united in a kind of liberty that

meant we could do whatever we wanted, anytime and anyplace, libertines would conflict with each other regarding the what, where, and how. We could be united again only in that Might would make Right. Unity via compulsion is not a desirable unity.

**Money ≠ Wealth:**

If the only wealth were money, inflation would melt away your nest egg. What could money buy if not another form of wealth? You would find it difficult to live in a house made of dollar bills. If money were distributed equally to enhance equity, that unity would last as long as no one had greater needs than another, or if no one wanted invest his/her money in the hopes of creating more.

**Idiosyncratic Behavior ≠ Idiotic Behavior**
**Mentally Erratic Behavior ≠ Just a Passionate Commitment:**

(Refer to License ≠ Liberty, above.) Imagine a free, equitable, unrestricted society in which you could not challenge any behavior on the grounds of insanity or even unsociability. People could act insanely (by current standards) and everyone else would have to accept their free expression. Unity, then, would equal chaos.

**Freely Expressed Opinions ≠ Valid Facts:**

Everyone is free to think what he/she wants. Thought creates reality only in the sense that thought is the root of creativity, and creativity can eventually mold what reality will look like. If simply having the thought, the opinion, or the point-of-view could change reality, however, it would mean that we would live in a psychedelic world, in which at each breath, each person could create a new reality. Hardly a state of unity.

**Being Offended ≠ Moral Superiority:**
Now let's all be offended equally! Such unity! But then who would do the offending? Okay then, let's all be morally superior. Morally superior to whom? You are more likely to be in consort with others if you are not easily offended nor take a stance of moral superiority.

**Climate Change ≠ Climate Crisis:**
If we all do everything recommended to save the planet in order to save ourselves from a climate catastrophe, we would impoverish millions, ruin economies, and relegate ourselves to a primitive state. To save ourselves, we'd have to destroy what keeps us alive. Whereas, if we deal with real concerns by first objectively determining that they are concerns, and second by making sure our responses would truly provide solutions, we can either eliminate a problem, diminish it, or at least delay a crisis.

**Journalism ≠ Reportage:**
If we believed everything we read in newspapers or saw on TV news, we would be wrong at least 50% of the time. Until real objective reporting returns, journalism has become akin to the weatherman who

lives in Hawaii and calls in his forecast for the rest of the country. To accept journalism as reportage is equivalent to accepting "experts" as accurate. That means people will have to accept being misinformed or disinformed in order to stay unified in their ignorance.

Rather than inventing new meanings to old terms or new terms that sound like old terms, let's understand our language so that we talk alike (and thus think via similar processes) and unify on the basis of common values. If we refuse to do so while believing what is easily refutable, we are choosing to live a lie.

No one was ever injured by the truth; but he who persists in self-deception and ignorance is injured.
Marcus Aurelius

# 16. Words Matter

In today's world, people argue that words matter because they are afraid of offending someone or being offended by those words. Sorry, folks, but in my humble opinion, "Sticks and stones, etc." While I appreciate Giuseppe taking care not to accidentally insult Maria, I take umbrage (yeah, that means I'm a little insulted) at the idea that Maria can claim any word, phrase, or sound as an intentional offense made to somehow "harm" her.

No one likes to be insulted, but if words really hurt a person, even according to that person's individual standards, no one could speak without potentially causing some sort of injury.

For me, words matter for a different reason. They matter because if you don't use them correctly or don't have an understanding of how someone may misuse them, you take the chance of accepting a falsehood as a truth. In other words, unconsciously you begin to live a lie, trying to mentally talk yourself into abiding by what you do not really believe.

Humans use words in every language in ways that are clever, creative, and often not literal. This is what can enrich a culture with both humor and emotive literature. In fact, Howard Nemerov (1920-1991), former Poet Laureate of the USA and a professor with whom I studied in college, advised his students to become familiar with puns in order to facilitate the *double entendres* and homonyms that would enrich our poetry writing. He did not live long enough to witness the creative use of language that would intentionally mislead and misinform, and not necessarily enrich, a society.

Because of the postmodernist influence in today's society, people claim there are no absolute truths, thus there can be no falsehoods. Everything is a matter of personal perspective or a perspective determined by your identity-bias. We are supposed to believe that somehow this relativistic orientation is not itself relative but absolute. Nothing is supposed to be objectively true except the "fact" that nothing is objectively true. And, if you don't believe that, you are a bigot (non-subjectively, of course) or sadly misinformed by the overarching powers of a controlling society. I think you are able to realistically assess whether you are bigoted or not, but probably less able to assess how the claim that you are bigoted (because you may not agree with a postmodernist point of view) can chip away at the stability of society.

If words help form our thinking, consider what sort of thinking you would prefer to form. In 1944, Ludwig von Mises, famed Austrian economist, wrote in *Omnipotent Government*: "Lenin was cynical enough to say that revolutions must be achieved with the catchwords of the day." Lenin knew that choice words were the key to people choosing how to think. Are the purveyors of cleverly conceived verbiage attempting a revolution? If so, it is *per force* a revolution of lies.

Later in the same book, von Mises writes:
...men enter into discussions, they speak to each other, they write letters and books, they try to prove or disprove. Social and intellectual cooperation between men would be impossible if this were not so. Our minds cannot even consistently imagine a world people[d] by men of different logical structures or a logical structure different from our own.

Yet, in the course of the nineteenth century this undeniable fact has been contested. Marx and Marxians [Marxists]...taught that thought is determined by the thinker's class position. What thinking produces is not truth but "ideologies." This word means, in the context of Marxian philosophy, a disguise of the selfish interests of the social class to which the thinking individual is attached. It is therefore useless to discuss anything with people other than social class.

Ideologies do not need to be refuted by discursive reasoning, they must be unmasked by denouncing the class position, the social background, of their authors. Thus Marxians do not discuss the merits of physical theories; they merely uncover the "bourgeois" origin of the physicists.

**But, dear author, it may be true that words can manipulate thought; however, words are often used to try to hurt people's feelings, as well! Why should we tolerate that? Words have been used to put down entire races, genders, and classes, have they not? Are you suggesting that insulting people by typing them as inferior because of their class, gender, or race is a good thing?**

No, not good thing, just not harmful enough to be illegal. Free speech means nothing if someone cannot say what you may not want to hear. People can claim to be "hurt" by truth as well as epithet. Ignoring demonstrable negative qualities in order to avoid the *accusation* of typing people is dangerous.

If a black woman is hired either because she is black or because she is a woman (or both), but is dangerously incompetent at her job, your saying that she is incompetent or even mildly incapable might be called Racist or Sexist. We are supposed to believe that your use of "incompetent" is more offensive, even if true, than someone calling you Racist or Sexist, although it is false. If we are too afraid to speak the truth, we will cower more when labeled anything negative. Rather than laughing at the absurdity, we cringe, not wanting others to consider us worse than what we ever could be on our worst day—on hallucinogens—after 24 hours of sleeplessness—driving across the Sahara—on a 1964 Vespa—naked. Why do we cower? Is it because we really don't know the truth when we see it, or because it is easier to conform to the wishes of those who make more emotionally insistent arguments?

They never consider truth or falsity when reacting to *your* alleged "insult" of the incompetent black woman. Since truth is irrelevant, they have no hesitation in pasting you with whatever label might hurt the most—simply to cause emotional distress, and thus get you to cave in. In this way, they prove to you that words matter. However, note that they never prove that truth matters. These are grade-school tactics. Whoever can come up with the most "painful" insult wins. Even in grade school, we are taught to say, "Sticks and stone will break my bones, but names will never hurt me." To play the game with them is to give in to the power of emotion-laden words and not to use truth as an arbiter. The danger is that we will go along to get along.

I can understand keeping a low profile for a while. If we go along to get along in order to reconnoiter or allow the opposition to overextend itself, fine. In that case, our hesitancy to speak up is a tactic.

However, if we simply retreat and passively accept new terminology, new definitions, and new ways of seeing the world simply because their advocates are loud, emotional, and insistent, we ignore the idea that neither "new" nor "emotional" nor "insistent" necessarily equals "desirable" or "correct". And, more importantly, we give up on the idea that an *objective* reality exists, whether or not people can perceive it equally.

Postmodernists, who do not believe in an objective reality, when they are not reacting with insults to those they think insensitive, use language specifically to sound "attractive", that is to convince, rather than to describe, identify, or relate to reality. Thus, by choosing the right, emotionally-charge words or phrases, a person influenced by postmodernism can easily make a listener draw connections that are not necessarily there. Intentional slight-of-phrase or emotional language is a way to take us off the main highway of reality onto the side road of deception, i.e. cheating ourselves into believing a false reality.

I once had a girlfriend who had lost her job and had two kids to take care of. She was forced to go on local welfare and was embarrassed about it. She strived to find employment as soon as possible so that she could get off the dole and earn her own money. Within two months, she did so, and within a year, became an assistant director in her new job. She had been embarrassed to take state aid, even under her circumstances, because she felt (1) she was victimizing taxpayers whose money she had not earned, and (2) she wanted always to earn her own way, never having to ask a for benefits not due to her. You might argue that welfare programs have been established precisely for her type of person, one who is in her type of situation, and she might even agree. However, there are those with fewer scruples who apply for welfare. It is easy for them to find a way to take advantage of the system, only a little of course, but then a little more, and then for an extended period of time. They are not incentivized to get off the dole as soon as possible; rather, they have been told that they have "welfare rights", so they are willing to believe that a certain sustenance is not a privilege of a generous society but is a benefit due them. Worse still is when those, who have decided to be professional recipients (in welfare or in politics), claim to be the *victims* of their cruel society! Thomas Sowell tells us, "You cannot subsidize irresponsibility and expect people to become more responsible." Both the welfare system and political employment dispense public money, thus both have to be well-patrolled. Misuse of either must result in consequences that are not simply "naughty children" slaps on the wrist. Anything less encourages irresponsibility at the minimum and fraud at the maximum.

Most people can recognize cheating when it comes to money but few recognize cheating when it comes to words. Consider the number of scam emails you receive every week. They are cleverly worded so that you think they just might be true. Their perpetrators don't expect every email recipient to fall for the scam, but they expect their careful imitation of reality will take in a small percentage of recipients and that small percentage will produce a large, unearned, and fraudulent profit.

Consider a phone pitch for a charity. Is it a real charity? If it is, how much of what you might contribute would actually go to the charity? Or is it all a cleverly worded phone presentation to have you send a check to a post office box for which you will receive a thank-you sticker to put on your car, proving what a generous and considerate person you are.

Not only are there con-men and con-women everywhere, but also the very tactics that they use have become ingrained in everyday salesmanship, and worse, everyday politics. Note how large, impossible-to-read bills have grandiose titles like "The Save America from Misinformation Bill". Five percent of it is about misinformation, and the rest fulfills the bill's sponsors' earmarks so that they can brag about how much they have benefitted their state or district.

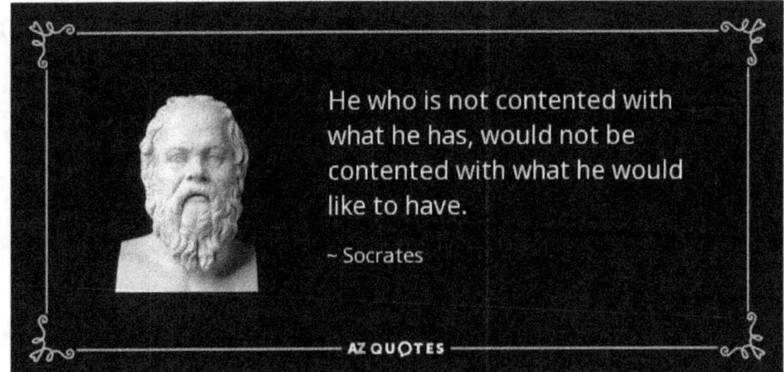


By using such tactics, we focus on appearance and feelings, not on actually accomplishing something that will solve a problem or benefit a constituency. We accept the idea that appearance is reality. Because appearance is not necessarily reality, we may go away temporarily placated, but never quite satisfied. And then the ploy is used again in order to fool us into thinking that this time we'll be satisfied, or at least a lot more satisfied, or may a little more satisfied, than before. Until next time.

It is not simply that we are being deceived much of the time; it is that we are participating in our own deception. We don't hold professionals to strict standards and we hold our politicians to none.  Postmodernists want us not to believe in objective truth. They want us to doubt the evidence of our senses most of the time, and our reasoning all of the time. They are essentially taking the true statement "What you see is not what you get" and making it much more absolute, so that it becomes something like, "Your senses deceive you" or "The real world cannot be trusted."

**Well, dear author, your senses *can* deceive you and the real world sometimes *cannot* be trusted, so why argue with this?**

I argue with the premise because it is not always true and yet the advocates of the postmodern point-of-view use it, when convenient, to make others doubt themselves and their ability to function in reality. If you cannot function in a world that you can understand, you will need help. There will be some postmodernist activist who will come to your rescue by offering "the real reality", as if you suddenly should ignore what they previously said about not trusting reality so you can unflinchingly believe whatever they tell you. This relegates you to a passive recipient of whatever life washes over you. In order not to be stressed about understanding life, you will accept a new convention, a convention that those who think they know put upon you. It will not be the drudgery of Orwell's *1984*, but the mindless "bliss" of Huxley's *Brave New World*. The Unity You Seek will not be The Unity You Get.

* * *

> '[It's] a dangerous conception of mental hygiene to assume that what man needs ... is equilibrium... . What man actually needs is not a tensionless state but rather a striving and struggling for a worthwhile goal...'
>
> – Viktor Frankl

As Above
So Below
/ If ignorance is bliss, why aren't more people happy? /
- Thomas Jefferson

# POSTSCRIPT: Other Inequalities To Think About

I did not include these in the text because they are not pure inequalities. Sometimes they are true, sometimes not. The error would be in automatically assuming that they are true. They are most easily read this way: "A does not always equal B" or "A does not necessarily equal B".

- New $\neq$ always Good
- Appearance $\neq$ always Reality
- What You See $\neq$ always What You Get
- Political Skills $\neq$ always Governing Skills
- Rhetorical Arguments $\neq$ always Valid Arguments
- A Vaccine $\neq$ always Immunity
- Happiness $\neq$ always Irresponsibility

But please do not take my word for all of this. I don't want to control you either directly or indirectly. I want you to control yourself based on the shared truth of human rationality, logic, and words having a clearly understood meaning based on their use in each circumstance.

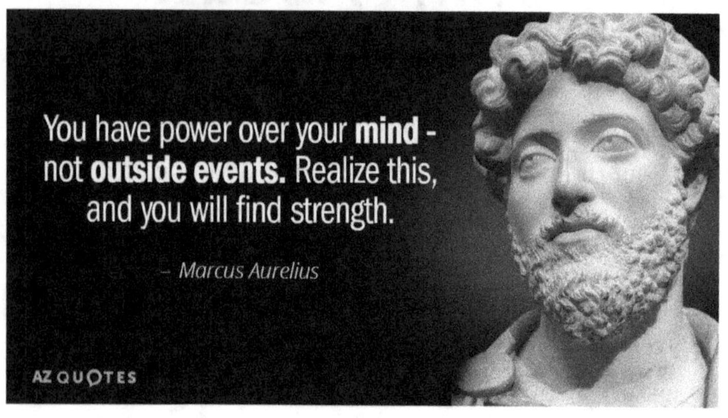

# The Little Book of In≠qualities
# BIBLIOGRAPHY


**AUDIO**

Sowell, Thomas, *Discrimination and Disparities*, Blackstone Audio, Inc., 2018

**BOOKS**

Annesi, Tony, *10 Common Values*, Amazon and B&N, 2019.
*Life is About Control*, Amazon and B&N, 2022.
*Petulant*, Amazon and B&N, 2020.
*Your Ethics Are Immoral*, Amazon and B&N, 2019.

Freedman, David H., *Wrong*, Little, Brown and Company, 2010.

Hicks, Stephen R. C., *Explaining Post-modernism*, Ockham's Razor Publishing, 2011.

Nichols, Tom, *The Death of Expertise*, Oxford University Press, 2017.

von Mises, Ludwig, *Omnipotent Government*, Liberty Fund, 1944, 1974

Windelband, Wilhelm, *A History of Philosophy, Volume II*, Harper Torchbook, 1958.

**WEBSITES**

*Climate:* https://www.anu.edu.au/news/
https://www.biznews.com/energy/2022/12/12/climate-crisis
https://www.biznews.com/global-citizen/2022/10/05/climate-change-2

https://Climate. Gov
https://www.epa.gov/ghgemissions/overview-green-house-gases
https://www.ncei.noaa.gov/access/monitoring/tornadoes/

*Experts/Ehrlich:* https://www.trivia-library.com/a/past-pre-dictions-by-famous-scientist-dr-paul-ehrlich.htm

*Logic:* https://arcapologetics.org/three-laws-logic/

*Kant:* https://plato.stanford.edu/entries/kant-moral/

*Post-modernism:* https://quizlet.com/6266751/8-tenets-of-postmodernism-flash-cards/

*Unity/Garibaldi:* https://www.thehistorycorner.org/articles-by-the-team/the-father-of-modern-italy-giuseppe-garib-aldi-and-the-italian-unification

# About the Author

Tony Annesi's writing falls into three categories:

(1) Instruction and Philosophy of Traditional Martial Arts,

(2) Fiction, including short stories and novels, and

(3) Cultural Commentary, of which this book is the seventh in the series.

His writing started with poetry and short fiction (the first stories of 1969: Loss of Innocence were drafted in 1969). He enhanced his martial arts career with columns for INSIDE KARATE MAGAZINE (*Tales of the Dojo* and *The Dojo Files*), and articles for MARTIAL

ARTS MASTERS, SELF-DEFENSE WORLD, IN-SIDE KUNG-FU, THE INTERNATIONAL FIGHTER, and BLACK BELT. He has authored *Cracking the Kata Code, The Road to Mastery, Principles of Advanced Budo, Sudden Attack Defense, Elevated Elementals, Comparative Aiki in Action,* and several volumes of essays called *Sunday with Sensei's Journal.*

In 2015, after 12 years of work, Tony completed a fantasy novel trilogy entitled *The Shangrilla Artifacts.* In 2018, he published the sequel, *An Atlantis of One.*

His books of social commentary include *10 Guideline Principles: Finding One's Way in a Messy World, 10 Common Values to Unify a Contentious Culture, Your Ethics Are Immoral, Petulant: How Pre-Feminist Peevishness and Guerrilla Warfare Has Poisoned Political Points of View, The Flaws of Freedom: Why the Left Depends on the Right and the Right Needs the Left, The Collective Problem vs. the Individualism Problem: the Challenge of Unforced Liberty,* and *Life is About Control: Responsibility vs. Domination.*

# Also by Tony Annesi in his
# CULTURAL COMMENTARY SERIES:

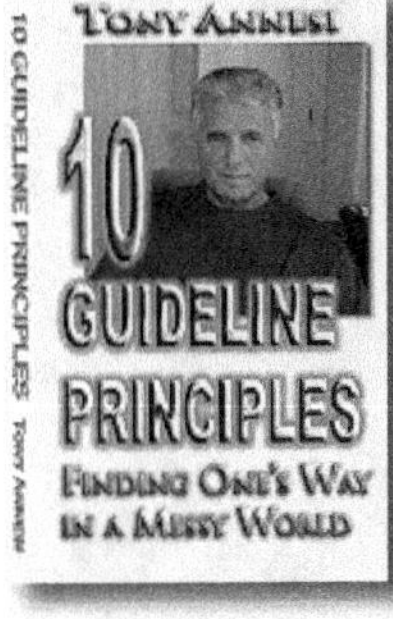

*Non-academic analysis and opinion for the average citizen who thinks about the world.*

9 798372 719910